Vienna

This book explores and debates the urban transformations that have taken place in Vienna over the past 30 years and their consequences in policy fields such as labour and housing, political and social participation and the environment. Historically, European cities have been characterised by a strong association between social cohesion, quality of life, economic ambition and a robust State. Vienna is an excellent example for that. In more recent years, however, cities were pressured to change policy principles and mechanisms in the context of demographic shifts, post-industrial transformations and welfare recalibration which have led to worsened social conditions in many cities. Each chapter in this volume discusses Vienna's responses to these pressures in key policy arenas, looking at outcomes from the context-specific local arrangements. Against a theoretical framework debating the European city as a model of inclusion and social justice, authors explore the local capacity to innovate urban policies and to address new social risks, while paying attention to potential trade-offs.

The book questions and assesses the city's resilience using time series and an institutional analysis of four key dimensions that characterise the European city model within the context of post-industrial transition: redistribution, recognition, representation and sustainability. It offers a multiscalar perspective of urban governance through labour, housing, participatory and environmental policies, bringing together different levels and public policy types.

Vienna: Still a Just City? is aimed at academics, researchers and policy-makers in urban studies, including urban sociology, ecology, geography and welfare.

Yuri Kazepov is a professor of International Urban Sociology and Compared Welfare Systems at the University of Vienna (Austria). Among his fields of interest are multilevel governance, the territorial dimension of social policies. On these issues, he has been carrying out comparative research and evaluation activities for the EU and National Agencies.

Roland Verwiebe is a professor of Social Stratification Research at the University of Potsdam (Germany). His research interests include the domains of social inequality, migration, attitudes and values as well as quality of life in the city. On these topics, he has published in leading international journals.

Built Environment City Studies

The *Built Environment City Studies* series provides researchers and academics with a detailed look at individual cities through a specific lens. These concise books delve into a case study of an international city, focusing on a key built environment topic. Written by scholars from around the world, the collection provides a library of thorough studies into trends, developments and approaches that affect our cities.

Rio de Janeiro
Urban Expansion and Environment
José L. S. Gámez, Zhongjie Lin and Jeffrey S Nesbit

Kuala Lumpur
Community, Infrastructure and Urban Inclusivity
Marek Kozłowski, Asma Mehan and Krzysztof Nawratek

Glasgow
High-Rise Homes, Estates and Communities in the Post-War Period
Lynn Abrams, Ade Kearns, Barry Hazley and Valerie Wright

Pemba
Spontaneous Living Spaces
Corinna Del Bianco

Vienna
Still a Just City?
Edited by Yuri Kazepov and Roland Verwiebe

For more information about this series, please visit: https://www.routledge.com/Built-Environment-City-Studies/book-series/BECS

Vienna
Still a Just City?

**Edited by
Yuri Kazepov and Roland Verwiebe**

First published 2022
by Routledge
4 Park Square, Milton Park, Abingdon, Oxon OX14 4RN

and by Routledge
605 Third Avenue, New York, NY 10158

Routledge is an imprint of the Taylor & Francis Group, an informa business

© 2022 selection and editorial matter, Yuri Kazepov and Roland Verwiebe; individual chapters, the contributors

The right of Yuri Kazepov and Roland Verwiebe to be identified as the authors of the editorial material, and of the authors for their individual chapters, has been asserted in accordance with sections 77 and 78 of the Copyright, Designs and Patents Act 1988.

The Open Access version of this book, available at www.taylorfrancis.com, has been made available under a Creative Commons Attribution-Non Commercial-No Derivatives 4.0 license.

Trademark notice: Product or corporate names may be trademarks or registered trademarks, and are used only for identification and explanation without intent to infringe.

British Library Cataloguing-in-Publication Data
A catalogue record for this book is available from the British Library

Library of Congress Cataloging-in-Publication Data
Names: Kazepov, Yuri, editor. | Verwiebe, Roland, editor.
Title: Vienna: still a just city? / edited by Yuri Kazepov and Roland Verwiebe.
Description: New York, NY: Routledge, 2022. | Series: Built environment city studies | Includes bibliographical references and index. | Identifiers: LCCN 2021041519 (print) | LCCN 2021041520 (ebook) | ISBN 9780367680114 (hardback) | ISBN 9780367680138 (paperback) | ISBN 9781003133827 (ebook)
Subjects: LCSH: Urban renewal—Austria—Vienna. | Vienna (Austria)—Economic conditions—21st century. | City planning—Environmental aspects—Austria—Vienna. | Dwellings—Social aspects—Austria—Vienna.
Classification: LCC HT178.A85 V54 2022 (print) | LCC HT178.A85 (ebook) | DDC 307.3/4160943613—dc23/eng/20211101
LC record available at https://lccn.loc.gov/2021041519
LC ebook record available at https://lccn.loc.gov/2021041520

ISBN: 978-0-367-68011-4 (hbk)
ISBN: 978-0-367-68013-8 (pbk)
ISBN: 978-1-003-13382-7 (ebk)

DOI: 10.4324/9781003133827

Typeset in Times New Roman
by codeMantra

Contents

List of figures	vii
List of tables	ix
List of contributors	xi

1 Is Vienna still a just city? The challenges of transitions   1
YURI KAZEPOV AND ROLAND VERWIEBE

PART I
Political participation   17

2 Still a red island? Vienna's electoral geography between stability and change   19
ELISABETTA MOCCA AND MICHAEL FRIESENECKER

3 Unlocking the door of the city hall: Vienna's participatory shift in urban development policy   35
BYEONGSUN AHN AND ELISABETTA MOCCA

PART II
Housing   51

4 Affordable housing for all? Challenging the legacy of Red Vienna   53
KATHARINA LITSCHAUER AND MICHAEL FRIESENECKER

5 Innovating social housing? Tracing the social in social housing construction   68
MICHAEL FRIESENECKER AND KATHARINA LITSCHAUER

PART III
Labour market 83

6 Between protection and activation: shifting
institutional arrangements and 'ambivalent' labour
market policies in Vienna 85
BYEONGSUN AHN AND YURI KAZEPOV

7 Professionalisation, polarisation or both? Economic
restructuring and new divisions of labour 99
BERNHARD RIEDERER, ROLAND VERWIEBE AND
BYEONGSUN AHN

PART IV
Environment 115

8 Vienna's urban green space planning: great stability
amid global change 117
ANNA-KATHARINA BRENNER, ELISABETTA MOCCA,
AND MICHAEL FRIESENECKER

9 Environmental quality for everyone? Socio-structural
inequalities in mobility, access to green spaces and air quality 131
MICHAEL FRIESENECKER, BERNHARD RIEDERER
AND ROBERTA CUCCA

10 Vienna's resilience: between urban justice and the
challenges ahead 146
ROLAND VERWIEBE, YURI KAZEPOV, MICHAEL
FRIESENECKER AND BYEONGSUN AHN

Index 159

Figures

2.1	Comparison of national and municipal elections: parties with most votes per districts, 1995–2020	23
2.2	Scatter plot for vote shares (2020) and satisfaction composite indicator (2018)	30
3.1	Institutional pathways to formal participation in urban development in Vienna	40
3.2	Geographical distribution of participatory channels in urban development in Vienna, 2020	45
4.1	Development of rental prices in sub-segments	62
4.2	Tenant profiles – income quintiles (2011, 2018) and citizenship (2005, 2018) across tenures in Vienna	64
5.1	Share of building permits for dwellings per developer in Vienna (%), 1980–2020	71
5.2	Distribution of municipal housing stock and new subsidised housing construction via developer competitions, 2020	72
6.1	Access to unemployment insurance in Austria and Vienna	91
6.2	Indexed growth of active and passive LMPs in Vienna, 2001–2019 (2001=100)	92
7.1	Development of the unemployment rate (national definition) in Vienna 2008–2020	105
7.2	Changes in the distribution of occupational classes in Vienna 1995–2019	107
8.1	Timeline of central UGS policies at different governing levels between 1905 and 2019	120
8.2	Availability of UGS per inhabitant, 2001 and 2018	126
9.1	Perceived quality of the living environment in Vienna (in %)	138

Tables

2.1	National elections: parties with most votes per federal states and capitals, 1990–2019	21
2.2	Correlation of vote shares for elections to district councils and satisfaction per district ($N=23$)	28
4.1	Tenure structure Vienna, 1991–2018	60
7.1	Employment in Vienna 1995–2019 (in %)	103
7.2	Determinants of occupational class in Vienna 1995 and 2019 (AME)	108
9.1	Regression models on perceived environmental quality	140

The research underlying this book was supported by the Austrian Science Fund (FWF) under the project: *Vienna in Transition. (Dis-)Continuities of Urban Change in a European City* (Project Number: P 30617). Open access costs have been covered by the FWF and the University of Potsdam.

Contributors

Editors

Yuri Kazepov is a professor of International Urban Sociology and Compared Welfare Systems at the University of Vienna (Austria). Among his fields of interest are multilevel governance, the territorial dimension of social policies. On these issues, he has been carrying out comparative research and evaluation activities for the EU and National Agencies.

Roland Verwiebe is a professor of Social Stratification Research at the University of Potsdam (Germany). His research interests include the domains of social inequality, migration, attitudes and values as well as quality of life in the city. On these topics, he has published in leading international journals.

Authors

Byeongsun Ahn is a researcher and a PhD candidate at the Department of Sociology at University of Vienna. He holds a BA in Political Science (University of Vienna) and an MSc in Sociology (University of Amsterdam). His research interests include everyday life, governance rescaling, path dependence, participatory planning and urban competitiveness.

Anna-Katharina Brenner is a researcher and a PhD candidate at the Institute of Social Ecology at the University of Natural Resources and Life Sciences (Austria). Among her fields of interest are environmental justice and the transition to urban sustainability. On these issues, she is carrying out interdisciplinary research considering both socio-metabolic and political/institutional implications.

xii *Contributors*

Roberta Cucca is an associate professor at the Norwegian University of Life Sciences, where she teaches Urban Sociology, and leads (with Jin Xue) the Urban Sustainability Research Group in the Department of Urban and Regional Planning. Her research interests are on the relationship between environmental policies and social vulnerability, social inequalities in contemporary cities and participation in local policy decision making.

Michael Friesenecker is a researcher at the Department of Sociology and a PhD candidate at the Department of Geography, University of Vienna. His recent research interests are urban (development) policies, neighbourhood revitalisation, gentrification and the social and spatial implications of housing and environmental policies.

Katharina Litschauer is a researcher at the Institute for Sociology and Social Research at WU Vienna (Austria). She holds an MA in Political Science (University of Vienna) and an MSc in Economics (WU Vienna). Her research interests include critical urban studies and political economy, whilst her scientific work centres on the social aspects of housing provision.

Elisabetta Mocca is a university post-doctoral assistant at the Department of Sociology, University of Vienna (Austria). Her research interests revolve around urban and territorial politics, political participation and environmental politics. On these topics she has published in leading international journals.

Bernhard Riederer is a postdoctoral researcher at the University of Vienna (Department of Sociology) and the Austrian Academy of Sciences (Vienna Institute of Demography). His work focuses on social inequality and family issues, usually involving regional and international comparisons (e.g. urban-rural differences in social stratification and fertility).

1 Is Vienna still a just city? The challenges of transitions

Yuri Kazepov and Roland Verwiebe

Introduction

Historically, European cities have been associated with social cohesion, quality of life and economic competitiveness, in particular since the Second World War (Kazepov, 2005). *Redistribution* (via generous social policies), *representation* (through democratic inclusion) and *recognition* (acknowledging diversity; Fraser et al., 2003) have all contributed to high levels of social justice (Fainstein, 2010). The strong influence of public (often national) institutions in urban development within Europe as a whole, including urban planning (Fincher and Iveson, 2008) and targeted national urban policies (Zimmermann and Fedeli, 2021), has led to local contexts characterised by lower levels of socio-spatial inequality and high standards of living in comparison to other cities throughout the world. Considering these traits as analytical building blocks, scholars have tended to identify the *European city* as a model of social justice (Le Galès, 2002; Häussermann, 2005). However, European cities are today under a great deal of pressure as a result of long-term transformations associated with the post-industrial transition, demographic trends, welfare rescaling and recalibration (Kazepov, 2010), and the effects of the 2008 economic and financial crisis, which has affected most European countries (and cities; Hemerijck, 2013). These trends have produced new social risks (e.g. structural long-term unemployment, new labour market vulnerabilities, etc.) that undermine the building blocks of the European city model, producing rising income vulnerabilities and poverty, discrimination of migrant populations and, in general, widening social and spatial inequalities within – but also between – cities (Novy and Mayer, 2009; Kazepov et al., 2021). Such transformations challenge the territorial cohesion of Europe and promote the emergence of different patterns of economic, political and social development across cities (Cassiers and Kesteloot, 2012; Lewis, 2017).

The magnitude of such changes and their impact, however, are not uniformly experienced and managed by European countries and cities (Brenner et al., 2010; Jessop, 2015; Le Galès, 2018), and there are varying degrees of resilience across respective localities. Recent investigations (Cucca and Ranci, 2017) highlight how such transformations bring about increasing differentiation among European cities, resulting from the interplay of structural factors, path dependencies and multilevel governance arrangements, on the one hand, and the ability of local institutions to deal with new social needs and problems, on the other. Some cities are better than others at innovating their policies in order to reduce the gap between emerging problems and financial constraints. Since the emergence of the economic crisis in 2008, the capacity to reduce these gaps could be interpreted as a measure of possible resilience (Fainstein, 2015), although questions as to why such differences are observable and what *makes a difference* remain open.

For this reason, we use the European city framework as a starting point in investigating how Vienna is addressing the challenges and consequences of new social risks. Vienna has been portrayed as highly representative of the European city model, having had a long history of promoting socially inclusive forms of urban development through specific social policy interventions and housing programmes. The roots of the *Vienna model* date back at least to the 1920s, a period known as *Red Vienna* (Blau, 1999; Kadi and Suitner, 2019), but continued throughout the post-war period as part of the corporatist welfare state model (Reinprecht, 2014; Österle and Heitzmann, 2020). However, due to ongoing population growth from the 1990s onwards, the impact of the financial crisis, austerity policies and the relatively recent refugee flows, Vienna is experiencing important pressures to orient its urban development strategies following stricter economic criteria. The housing sector has faced particular pressures due to changes in rent regulation (Kadi, 2015; Friesenecker and Kazepov, 2021). However, systematic empirical analyses of relevant shifts in urban, housing and welfare policies and their implications for Vienna have so far remained scarce. Existing studies limit themselves to examining specific local policies or focus only on certain areas of the city and have not explicitly addressed the city in all its dimensions (with exceptions: Matznetter, 1990; Novy et al., 2001; Musil, 2009). In this multifaceted book, we aim at contributing towards filling this gap, presenting the results of our ongoing investigations regarding change in four relevant domains: (a) political representation; (b) housing; (c) labour market and (d) the environment. Change in these areas has had important consequences for the degree of social inclusion of inhabitants of the city.

The European city and justice: theoretical debates

During the Fordist period, cities in Europe were the centre of both production and consumption, fuelling economic growth and requiring the organisation of social reproduction through stable industrial relations and redistributive policies (e.g. welfare and housing). Such measures, which gave protection to vulnerable groups, made living in the city more affordable. The acceleration of global economic restructuring, kicked off by the economic crises of the 1970s and the shift towards post-industrial urban economies from the 1980s onwards, has impacted the local urban conditions and inequalities in cities worldwide, including Europe (OECD, 2018). Following these transitions, economic flexibility has become prioritised over social stability, and the search for greater competitiveness was no longer connected to a high level of social integration (Cucca and Ranci, 2017). The 2008 economic crisis brought about deeper welfare state recalibration (if not retrenchment) in most European countries, challenging redistributive policies (Hemerijck, 2013), which substantiate formal recognition of rights and social justice struggles at the city level (Fainstein, 2010).

Academic discussions surrounding urban transformation have largely been shaped by two main theoretical approaches, and complemented by a third, emergent, one: (1) a structural neo-Marxist approach, which considers economic dynamics to be the most relevant driver of change, and regards a neoliberal turn in contemporary cities as a spatial fix, functional to the post-industrial and global restructuring of capitalist society (Brenner et al., 2010); (2) a neo-Weberian approach, which highlights the capacity of European cities to govern social and economic transformations and combine strategies to promote competitiveness with consideration for locally based, collective interests (Bagnasco and Le Galès, 2000; Le Galès, 2002); and (3) an approach characterised by the concept of urban justice and resilience that – in its different forms – attempts to combine the previous two approaches by showing, on the one hand, the importance of claims to *the right of the city* (Lefebvre, 1968) as well as the role of urban contention; and on the other hand, the importance of institutions and rights in substantiating justice. Important differences exist among cities in this regard, and they need to be embedded in specific, multilevel governance arrangements which frame context-specific outcomes.

1   *The structural neo-Marxist approach.* International urban studies research has highlighted the rising importance of how developments in the global economy, seemingly *exogenous* to local

policymaking and governance, have gained significance for urban development trajectories. Concepts such as 'dual cities', 'global cities', and 'divided cities' draw close connections between global economic forces and changes in the local social and economic urban order (Harvey, 1989; Sassen, 1991; Andreotti et al., 2018). The crisis of Fordism led to a roll-back of redistributive politics and a roll-out of entrepreneurial governance (Harvey, 1989; Peck and Tickell, 2002). Thus, a fundamental political reorientation towards global competitiveness – through the processes of deregulation and privatisation – was set in motion globally and discussed through the analytical lens of neoliberalism (Brenner et al., 2010; for a crique: Le Galès, 2016). New modes of governance and the pressure for competitiveness brought about strategies that focused on large-scale cultural, political and sporting events, the desire to create culture-led (Kalandides, 2013) or 'green' (Garcia-Lamarca et al., 2021), and city-branding strategies, all of which can be seen as efforts to create new 'fixes' for capital accumulation. Moreover, housing is increasingly dominated by the interests of private – often (global) financialised – capital (Aalbers, 2017). These changes resulted in the visible increase in inequality within urban areas, which has been captured throughout the 1990s in the American context as 'dual or divided cities' (Mollenkopf and Castells, 1991; Fainstein, 1995). Also, in recent decades, processes of gentrification and segregation have been documented in European cities, although in variegated forms (Musterd et al., 2017; Arbaci, 2018). This corresponds to an urban labour market, which is almost entirely service oriented, thus fuelling a polarisation of occupational composition (Sassen, 1991; Burgers and Musterd, 2002; Pratschke and Morlicchio, 2012; Storper, 2018). Regarding political participation, Swyngedouw speaks of a 'post-political urban order', in which a post-democratic arrangement 'has replaced debate, disagreement and dissent with a series of technologies of governing that fuse around consensus, agreement, accountancy metrics and technocratic environmental management' (Swyngedouw, 2009, p.601). Thus, democratic relations are fundamentally becoming eroded (Crouch, 2004; Leitner et al., 2007; Mayer, 2013), as the post-political order 'dismantles welfare systems, increases inequality, and unleashes into urban political life the harsh relations of market competition' (Purcell, 2009, p.143). Pressed by the effects of austerity measures, emerging social needs induced by the mood of permanent crisis – as if *there is no alternative* – municipalities are increasingly bundling resources and cutting (or tightening access to) welfare services. This trend brings about claims and conflicts revolving around the *right to the city* (Lefebvre, 1968), which has inspired social movements demanding, for example, participation in planning, environmental protection and the provision of affordable housing.

2   *The neo-Weberian approach.* The previous line of reasoning has been criticised by scholars closer to a neo-Weberian approach, particularly with regard to the overly universalising claims in most global cities research (Bagnasco and Le Galès, 2000; Le Galès, 2002). Specifically, what is called into question is the failure to acknowledge the persistence of distinctive national and local institutional arrangements in light of more global economic shifts (Marcuse and van Kempen, 2000; Obinger et al., 2011). Advocates of this approach call for an analysis of redistributive institutions at different scales and of their role in shaping urban change and social transformation (Kazepov, 2010). Essentially, this neo-institutional literature has highlighted the continued significance of welfare and redistributive policies – including housing, as well as labour market and educational programmes – in mediating the impacts of global economic restructuring at the local and regional level. In particular, European cities retain distinctive governance features and comparatively low levels of social and spatial inequalities (Musterd and Ostendorf, 1998). These specific characteristics, and the period of relative demographic and economic growth that characterised many (West-) European cities up until the crisis unfolded in 2008, revived a discourse in the scholarly literature on the renaissance of 'the European city' (Kazepov et al., 2021). However, this approach retains some degree of vagueness, not always accounting for intra-European differences (Novy and Mayer, 2009). Moreover, it does not take account of East European cities, where the process of transformation since 1989 became more challenging, especially because social policies were severely and abruptly resized (Ferenčuhová and Gentile, 2016).

3   *An urban justice and resilience approach.* The previous approaches produced fairly articulated debates about how to put the question of justice in the city at the core of their struggles. Ranging from more Marxist approaches, contesting neoliberalism and mobilising for the right to the city against the urbanisation of injustice (Merrifield and Swyngedouw, 1996), to specific strands of the neo-Weberian approach, addressing the combination of social justice and resilience in cities through the workings of institutions (Le Galès, 2018). Bridging these two perspectives, Fainstein's

concept of the *'just city'* links critique of global and neoliberal developments, local policies and changes of the urban fabric with their redistributive consequences. Fainstein (2010) assumes certain room for manoeuvre for local and national policy in defining urban development trajectories and living conditions in times of rising global interconnectedness. The implicit argument in focusing on the concept of resilience is that when unavoidable events lead to system change, these very systems will show different levels of capacity to adapt and/or reconfigure their structure in order to maintain an acceptable growth path in output, employment and wealth in the long run. Although this approach has been criticised for being functionalist and because it obfuscates underlying conflicts and the distribution of benefits resulting from policy choices (Fainstein, 2015), we consider it useful to connect aspects related to urban justice, the challenges of changes and social and institutional innovation. It is an approach that can be complemented by an emphasis on the role of policy instruments in the overall governance of urban change (Kassim and Le Galès, 2010). Indeed, principles of justice do translate into policy measures, which not only define the regulatory framework within which actors unfold their struggles, but also provide them with resources, rights and duties, opportunities and constraints (Knijn and Lepianka, 2020).

The wide spectrum of approaches that have been developed within international urban research all bear some elements of truth in the analysis of how cities change in the 21st century. In this book, we want to contribute to this debate using Vienna as a case in point. We also want to move forward from the existing fragmentation of research on Vienna by analysing how the city has changed over the last 30 years (1989–2019), referring to these debates and attempting to integrate the various approaches without theoretical prejudice.

Between structural changes and institutional responses

Vienna has a long history of promoting socially inclusive forms of urban development through specific redistributive policy interventions, making it relevant not only for debates within the framework of the *European city* but also in terms of urban justice and emerging local forms of citizenship. While other cities (e.g. London, Paris, Berlin or Amsterdam) have long been at the centre of the debate, Vienna has only recently been the subject of more scholarly attention, and this tends to be predominantly in the field of housing. Here, Vienna aimed to counterbalance market processes with progressive redistributive policies for promoting social equality, be it through the direct construction of social housing by the municipality, the funding of affordable housing provision through limited-profit associations, comprehensive rent regulation and active land banking policies (Reinprecht, 2014; Friesenecker and Kazepov, 2021). The interest in Vienna, however, goes beyond housing. As we will see, other policy domains have relied on similar regulatory principles, fostering social justice and inclusion, trying to complement or compensate for policies developed at the federal level (e.g. on the labour market) and supra-national levels (e.g. on participation and the environment) to enhance the degree of inclusiveness at the city level.

Has this situation changed in the last three decades? As with most cities, Vienna has undergone important socio-economic and demographic structural changes in that time that have challenged the patterns of social justice developed after the Second World War. From a socio-economic point of view, the shift from the industrial sector to the service sector has accelerated in the last three decades, showing a marked tertiarisation. These trends have been accompanied by significant changes in the structure of the population. In fact, despite an ageing native population and a low birth rate, net in-migration has contributed to an increase in inhabitants, by around 350,000 since the year 2000, so that the population reached 1.91 million in 2020 and is expected to grow further still (https://bit.ly/2TjOlS7). These changes were partly the result of Austria joining the European Union in 1995 and of the EU expanding eastwards between 2004 and 2007. This repositioned Vienna from the fringes of a divided Europe into the heart of an 'integrating' economic and political space bridging East and West (Musil, 2009; Novy, 2011).

The joint effect of these changes produced negative intersectionalities, socio-economic insecurity and rising unemployment, in particular among unqualified school leavers. The consequences of these developments and their synergic effects with other changes are yet to be fully investigated for the city. However, are institutional arrangements and policies addressing these challenges adequately? A number of studies have highlighted an emerging social divide in the city, spatialising social stratification patterns (Hatz et al., 2016). These range from top-down recommodification processes of housing through legal changes and deregulation (Novy et al., 2001; Kadi, 2015) to increasingly segregated migrant economies (Kohlbacher and Reeger, 2016; Riederer et al., 2019), the exclusion of specific groups from political participation (Ehs, 2018) and uneven access to urban green spaces and public transportation

(Haslauer et al., 2015). As we will see in detail through the various chapters of this book, policies in the areas of housing, labour market, political participation, and the environment filter the impact of the changes in peculiar ways and influence the recognition of rights, redistributive outcomes and participatory arrangements. Will Vienna be able to govern these challenges? What conclusions can be reached for an international urban research agenda from an analysis of Vienna's specificities? Is a new insider-outsider divide emerging and – if so – along which lines? Are new and old inequalities stratifying in specific ways?

Aim and structure of this book

Despite the fact that Vienna represents a prime example of a European city under growing pressure, no systematic and conceptually encompassing research has yet investigated the role of institutional frameworks across policy domains in shaping urban inequalities and social conditions in the city. In order to bring the fragmented landscape of existing research together, each chapter of this book will carry out a thematic analysis of the interactions among the three key analytical dimensions characterising the overlapping debates regarding *the European city* and social justice: (a) the role of redistribution policies; (b) the recognition of rights and diversity; and (c) the role of political representation. These dimensions will be empirically analysed, focusing on four areas: (1) political participation and governance; (2) labour market policies; (3) access to housing and its affordability; and (4) environmental justice.

Each individual chapter aims to identify any potential trade-offs and synergic effects that have emerged over the last three decades (1989–2019), potentially impacting upon the degree of inclusiveness of the city. In doing so, the chapters relate the four policy areas to the respective contextual and institutional conditions and any change over time. By doing so, they show the interplay across the multiple territorial jurisdictions within which the city acts, draws resources, and plays out conflicts, thus disentangling the governance dynamics that are taking place. This long-term perspective allows us to identify how the potential contradictions and conflicts between neoliberal economic change and the capacity to govern social and economic transformations play out in the city. We can then explore whether it is possible to combine socially inclusive policies, environmental protection and (socially) innovative initiatives with economic competitiveness, and if so, to explore which preconditions are necessary as well as any divides that are emerging.

Is Vienna still a just city? 9

The chapters provide a systematic, comprehensive analysis of the analytical dimensions identified above, providing the reader with the building blocks with which to reconstruct Vienna's overall profile. Accordingly, the book is divided into four sections, each addressing the four respective policy areas, with two chapters for each. The themes analysed in each chapter are aimed at highlighting how the transformations taking place throughout the last 30 years have influenced the degree of inclusion proffered by the city.

1 *Political participation and governance.* In order to understand democratic processes and the extent of social justice in the city, it is important to disentangle how people maintain control over their living environments. From this point of view, Vienna represents a unique case: since the foundation of the Austrian Republic in 1919, the city government has been controlled by the Social Democratic Party (SPÖ), the Nazi period being the only exception. As Chapter 2 shows, this has been an important factor in shaping the recognition of social rights and redistribution of resources, through generous provision of city-specific services and benefits that have influenced patterns of social justice in the city and the consensus of its inhabitants. Over the last few decades, calls for more democratic control of decision-making in city planning have arisen, and a strong request for social participation to complement the representative democracy (Fainstein, 2010; Silver et al., 2010). In Vienna, as Chapter 3 shows, this process has occurred predominantly from the top-down, even when decentralisation brought about localised collaborative arrangements. In fact, the corporatist governance system formalised spaces for public-private-citizen partnerships between the administration and non-institutional actors at the neighbourhood level. As the two chapters show, the role of the public sector is crucial to understanding justice patterns in the city, relying on redistribution more than on bottom-up democratic participatory processes.

2 *Access to housing, affordability and innovation.* Housing has been a key area for neoliberal attacks on welfare state regulation. The transformation of housing markets, however, differs strongly from context to context (Scanlon et al., 2014). Several national and municipal authorities have abolished rent regulations and sold off public-owned dwellings, reducing affordable housing solutions for the lower- and middle-class populations. As Chapters 4 and 5 show, Vienna still displays a high degree of resilience, and the long tradition of affordable housing policies has

never been significantly discontinued, even though recognition and redistribution underwent important changes. Some authors have started to recognise an increasing dualisation (Kadi, 2015; Friesenecker and Kazepov, 2021); in particular, as far as access to affordable housing for newcomers in the city (especially ethnic minorities groups) is concerned. In fact, despite widening access to council housing, access is ultimately limited by long waiting lists, and non-profit units require a substantial down-payment by tenants. Additionally, the national government has progressively liberalised rent regulation in the private rental market. In this context, housing prices have also substantially increased in Vienna – especially for new residents – albeit from a much lower level than other capital cities, such as Amsterdam, Berlin, Paris or Zurich. The aim of the two housing chapters is to present how the potential insider-outsider divide plays out in Vienna, which mechanisms challenge the inclusiveness of housing policies in the city, and highlighting the potential innovative and institutional responses to these trends.

3   *Labour markets, occupational restructuring and policies.* European cities have exhibited different trends in their general transition from a Fordist economic structure to a service-based economy (Koch, 2006). In Chapters 6 and 7, the authors seek to capture the features of this transition in Vienna, and to analyse how the occupational structure has changed, with which effects and how policies have co-evolved. This aspect seems to gain particular relevance in the local debate within Vienna, where unemployment has been presented as a challenge to social stability and cultural identity, polarising public opinion and putting the educational system of the city, social services and active labour market policies under pressure (Atzmüller, 2009). These chapters show who is affected most by the post-Fordist transition of the productive system of the region and how policies have responded to the challenges. The degree of freedom Vienna retains as a *Bundesland* has allowed the City to develop a partly autonomous labour market policy, complementing and compensating for the impact of structural changes and federal labour market reforms. This has allowed Vienna to preserve, to a great extent, high levels of inclusion.

4   *Environmental justice and sustainability.* Policies implemented to address the challenges of environmental change are important when urban resilience and justice are investigated. As we will see in Chapters 8 and 9, the City of Vienna tries to balance an environmentally friendly context, competitiveness in the global market

Is Vienna still a just city? 11

and social inclusiveness. Balancing these dimensions, however, is not easy. In these two chapters, the authors engage critically with the potential trade-offs in the provision of access to urban green spaces and high-quality environments. Disentangling any potential contradictions, the authors illustrate how green policies can introduce inequalities if the social dimension is not considered in the equation. Indeed, they highlight how, by keeping the governance of environmental issues under the jurisdiction of the city's government, Vienna has been able to influence both access to, and distribution of, urban green spaces across social classes following an equity principle. This is evident also in the increasing and widespread perceptions of environmental quality in the city. Inequalities, however, do exist and persist, particularly for some foreign-born groups who cumulate several disadvantages (from housing to the labour market). In recent years, awareness has increased with regard to the fact that, in pursuing social *and* environmental justice, the integration of different policy domains is required.

The clear challenge that emerges from the analysis of these four areas is the relevance of the insider/outsider divide and the ambiguity of how it has been structured over recent decades. This challenge exists in every jurisdiction that has the power to intervene and modify the boundary-making process and define the criteria of who is *in* and who is *out*. However, it is even more apparent in cities, considering the decentralisation/devolution trends from the 1980s onwards. Vienna is in a privileged position in this regard since it is both a city and a regional government in a federal state which grants its *Bundesländer* a relatively high degree of autonomy and resources. The chapters of this book collectively show how the City of Vienna has used its (delegated) political power to influence the way in which the boundaries of justice and equity and the inclusionary/exclusionary dynamic have been redrawn (Knijn and Lepianka, 2020). The strong role of the public sector – and the inherent resilience of institutions – have mitigated the impact of neoliberal tendencies, not only slowing down the processes of change but also buying time to experiment with innovative solutions (most prominently in housing, but similarly on the labour market). This overall tendency has not prevented exclusionary processes, and some social groups are more affected than others: for instance, the substantial immigration of recent years has caused newcomers to experience more difficulties in accessing housing compared to long-term residents; lower educated newcomers have even more difficulty in finding a job on the labour market than those who are more highly educated, and so on. The magnitude of these gaps, however, is surely smaller than in other cities, and Vienna can still be considered a city in which recognition and redistribution play an important role. Participatory practices are still in their infancy, but growing, and attempts to combine social and environmental justice are advancing on the political agenda.

Acknowledgements and thanks

The quality of research and writing relies on many factors. Not insignificant in this case was the part played by the members of the advisory board of the 'Vienna in Transition' project: Talja Blokland, Susan Fainstein, Chris Hamnett, Håkan Johansson, Thomas Madreiter, Enzo Mingione, John Mollenkopf and Sako Musterd. In addition to providing substantial feedback on methods, content and argument, they also commented upon the individual chapters and engaged in discussion with all authors. It was a real privilege being able to rely on such scholarship. Thomas Madreiter was also able to involve officials from the City of Vienna who gave ad hoc feedback on the single thematic chapters. In particular, Clemens Horak, Isabel Wieshofer, Tobias Troger, Bruno Sagmeister, Daniel Glaser, Edith Waltner and Wencke Hertzsch should receive much thanks for their precise and valuable input. We also highly appreciate the support of Ramon Bauer from the Statistics Department of the City of Vienna (MA23), who facilitated our access to data. James Connolly, Luigino Ceccarini, Fabio Bordignon and Ilvo Diamanti helped with comments on specific chapters. Besides the content, we enjoyed the language proofreading of Emma Hewitt and the editorial work of Nina Görgen and Sebastian Harnacker, who substantially improved the manuscript. Lisa Finocchiaro supported us from an administrative point of view throughout the whole editorial project. Finally, we would also like to thank the authors of the chapters for their patience and for engaging with our never-ending comments: the quality of the output is a shared responsibility.

References

Aalbers, M.B., 2017. The variegated financialization of housing. *International Journal of Urban and Regional Research*, 41(4), pp. 542–554.

Andreotti, A., Benassi, D. and Kazepov, Y., eds., 2018. *Western capitalism in transition: Global processes, local challenges*. Manchester: Manchester University Press.

Arbaci, S., 2018. *Paradoxes of segregation: Housing systems, welfare regimes and ethnic residential change in southern European cities.* Hoboken, NJ: John Wiley & Sons.

Atzmüller, R., 2009. Institution building and active labour market policies in Vienna since the 1990s. *International Journal of Sociology and Social Policy*, 29(11/12), pp. 599–611.

Bagnasco, A. and Le Galès, P., eds., 2000. *Cities in contemporary Europe.* Cambridge: Cambridge University Press.

Blau, E., 1999. *The architecture of red Vienna, 1919–1934.* Cambridge, MA: The MIT Press.

Brenner, N., Peck, J. and Theodore, N., 2010. Variegated neoliberalization: Geographies, modalities, pathways. *Global Networks*, 10(2), pp. 182–222.

Burgers, J. and Musterd, S., 2002. Understanding urban inequality: A model based on existing theories and an empirical illustration. *International Journal of Urban and Regional Research*, 26(2), pp. 403–413.

Cassiers, T. and Kesteloot, C., 2012. Socio-spatial inequalities and social cohesion in European cities. *Urban Studies*, 49(9), pp. 1909–1924.

Crouch, C., 2004. *Post-democracy.* Cambridge: Polity Press.

Cucca, R. and Ranci, C., eds., 2017. *Unequal cities: The challenge of post-industrial transition in times of austerity.* London and New York: Routledge.

Ehs, T., 2018. *Wien wählt (nicht): Demokratische Beteiligung 1918–2018.* [pdf] Available at: https://bit.ly/34ouYcI [Accessed 27 May 2021].

Fainstein, S., ed., 1995. *Divided cities: New York & London in the contemporary world.* Oxford: Blackwell.

Fainstein, S., 2010. *The just city.* Ithaca, NY: Cornell University Press.

Fainstein, S., 2015. Resilience and Justice. *International Journal of Urban and Regional Research*, 39(1), pp. 157–167.

Ferenčuhová, S. and Gentile, M., 2016. Introduction: Post-socialist cities and urban theory. *Eurasian Geography and Economics*, 57(4–5), pp. 483–496.

Fincher, R. and Iveson, K., 2008. *Planning and diversity in the city: Redistribution, recognition and encounter.* Basingstoke: Palgrave Macmillan.

Fraser, N., Honneth, A. and Golb, J., 2003. *Redistribution or recognition? A political-philosophical exchange.* London: Verso.

Friesenecker, M. and Kazepov, Y., 2021. Housing Vienna: The socio-spatial effects of inclusionary and exclusionary mechanisms of housing provision. *Social Inclusion*, 9(2), pp. 77–90.

Garcia-Lamarca, M., Anguelovski, I., Cole, H., et al., 2021. Urban green boosterism and city affordability: For whom is the 'branded' green city? *Urban Studies*, 58(1), pp. 90–112.

Harvey, D., 1989. *The condition of postmodernity: An enquiry into the origins of cultural change.* Malden, MA: Blackwell.

Haslauer, E., Delmelle, E.C., Keul, A., et al., 2015. Comparing subjective and objective quality of life criteria: Case study of green space and public transport in Vienna, Austria. *Social Indicators Research*, 124(3), pp. 911–927.

Hatz, G., Kohlbacher, J. and Reeger, U., 2016. Socio-economic segregation in Vienna: A social-oriented approach to urban planning and housing. In: Tammaru, T., Marcinczak, S., van Ham, M. and Musterd, S., eds., 2016. *Socio-economic segregation in European capital cities: East meets west.* London and New York: Routledge, pp. 80–109.

Häussermann, H., 2005. The end of the European City? *European Review*, 13(2), pp. 237–249.

Hemerijck, A., 2013. *Changing welfare states.* Oxford: Oxford University Press.

Jessop, B., 2015. Comparative capitalisms and/or variegated capitalism. In: Ebenau, M. and May, C., eds., 2015. *New directions in comparative capitalisms research: Critical and global perspectives.* Basingstoke: Palgrave Macmillan, pp. 65–82.

Kadi, J., 2015. Recommodifying housing in formerly "Red" Vienna? *Housing, Theory and Society*, 32(3), pp. 247–265.

Kadi, J. and Suitner, J., 2019. Red Vienna, 1919–1934. In: Orum, A.M., García, M., Judd, D.R., Pow, C.-P. and Roberts, B.R., eds., 2019. *The Wiley-Blackwell encyclopedia of urban and regional studies:* Chichester, West Sussex: Wiley Blackwell, pp. 1–5.

Kalandides, A., ed., 2013. The business of place: Critical, practical and pragmatic perspectives. *Journal of Place Management and Development*, 6(1).

Kassim, H. and Le Galès, P., 2010. Exploring governance in a multi-level polity: A policy instruments approach. *West European Politics*, 33(1), pp. 1–21.

Kazepov, Y., ed., 2005. *Cities of Europe: Changing contexts, local arrangements, and the challenge to urban cohesion.* Malden, MA: Blackwell Publishing.

Kazepov, Y., ed., 2010. *Rescaling social policies: Towards multilevel governance in Europe.* Farnham, Surrey: Ashgate.

Kazepov, Y., Cucca, R., Ahn, B., et al., 2021. European cities between continuity and change. In: Orum, A.M., Ruiz-Tagle, J. and Vicari Haddock, S., eds., 2021. *Companion to urban and regional studies.* Hoboken, NJ: John Wiley & Sons, pp. 107–132.

Knijn, T. and Lepianka, D., eds., 2020. *Justice and vulnerability in Europe: An interdisciplinary approach.* Cheltenham, UK and Northampton, MA: Edward Elgar Publishing.

Koch, M., 2006. *Roads to post-fordism: Labour market and social structures in Europe.* Aldershot: Ashgate.

Kohlbacher, J. and Reeger, U., 2016. Business activities of immigrants from Turkey and the former Yugoslavia in Vienna. *City*, 20(1), pp. 101–115.

Le Galès, P., 2002. *European cities: Social conflicts and governance.* Oxford: Oxford University Press.

Le Galès, P., 2016. Neoliberalism and urban change: Stretching a good idea too far? *Territory, Politics, Governance*, 4(2), pp. 154–172.

Le Galès, P., 2018. Urban political economy beyond convergence: Robust but differentiated unequal European cities. In: Andreotti, A., Benassi, D. and

Kazepov, Y., eds., 2018. *Western capitalism in transition: Global processes, local challenges.* Manchester: Manchester University Press, pp. 217–236.

Lefebvre, H., 1968. *Le droit à la ville.* Paris: Anthropos.

Leitner, H., Peck, J. and Sheppard, E.S., 2007. *Contesting neoliberalism: Urban frontiers.* New York: Guilford Press.

Lewis, J., 2017. Inequalities in European Cities. In: Isaacs, S., ed., 2017. *European social problems:* London and New York: Routledge Taylor & Francis Group, pp. 71–94.

Marcuse, P. and van Kempen, R., eds., 2000. *Globalizing cities: A new spatial order?* Oxford: Blackwell.

Matznetter, W., 1990. What kind of privatization? The case of social housing in Vienna, Austria. *Journal of Housing and the Built Environment*, 5(2), pp. 181–197.

Mayer, M., 2013. First world urban activism. *City*, 17(1), pp. 5–19.

Merrifield, A. and Swyngedouw, E., 1996. *The urbanization of injustice.* London: Lawrence & Wishart.

Mollenkopf, J.H. and Castells, M., eds., 1991 *Dual city: Restructuring New York.* New York: Russell Sage Foundation.

Musil, R., 2009. Global capital control and city hierarchies: an attempt to reposition Vienna in a world city network. *Cities*, 26(5), pp. 255–265.

Musterd, S., Marcińczak, S., van Ham, M., et al., 2017. Socioeconomic segregation in European capital cities. Increasing separation between poor and rich. *Urban Geography*, 38(7), pp. 1062–1083.

Musterd, S. and Ostendorf, W., 1998. *Urban segregation and the welfare state: Inequality and exclusion in Western cities.* London: Routledge.

Novy, A., 2011. Unequal diversity – on the political economy of social cohesion in Vienna. *European Urban and Regional Studies*, 18(3), pp. 239–253.

Novy, A., Redak, V., Jäger, J., et al., 2001. The end of Red Vienna. *European Urban and Regional Studies*, 8(2), pp. 131–144.

Novy, J. and Mayer, M., 2009. As just as it gets? The European City in the Just City discourse. In: Marcuse, P., Connolly, J., Novy, J., Olivo, I., Potter, C. and Steil, J., eds., 2009. *Searching for the just city: Debates in urban theory and practice.* London and New York: Routledge.

Obinger, H., Starke, P., Moser, J., et al., 2011. *Transformations of the welfare state: Small states, big lessons.* Oxford: Oxford University Press.

OECD, 2018. *OECD regions and cities at a glance 2018.* Paris: OECD.

Österle, A. and Heitzmann, K., 2020. Austrification in welfare system change? An analysis of welfare system developments in Austria between 1998 and 2018. In: Blum, S., Kuhlmann, J. and Schubert, K., eds., 2020. *Routledge handbook of European welfare systems:* London: Routledge, pp. 21–37.

Peck, J. and Tickell, A., 2002. Neoliberalizing space. *Antipode*, 34(3), pp. 380–404.

Pratschke, J. and Morlicchio, E., 2012. Social polarisation, the labour market and economic restructuring in Europe: An urban perspective. *Urban Studies*, 49(9), pp. 1891–1907.

Purcell, M., 2009. Resisting neoliberalization: Communicative planning or counter-hegemonic movements? *Planning Theory*, 8(2), pp. 140–165.

Reinprecht, C., 2014. Social housing in Austria. In: Scanlon, K., Whitehead, C.M.E. and Arrigoitia, M.F., eds., 2014. *Social housing in Europe:* Chichester, West Sussex: Wiley Blackwell, pp. 61–73.

Riederer, B., Verwiebe, R. and Seewann, L., 2019. Changing social stratification in Vienna: Why are migrants declining from the middle of society? *Population, Space and Place*, 25(2), p.e2215.

Sassen, S., 1991. *The global city: New York, London, Tokyo.* Princeton, NJ: Princeton University Press.

Scanlon, K., Whitehead, C.M.E. and Arrigoitia, M.F., eds., 2014. *Social housing in Europe.* Chichester, West Sussex: Wiley Blackwell.

Silver, H., Scott, A. and Kazepov, Y., 2010. Participation in urban contention and deliberation. *International Journal of Urban and Regional Research*, 34(3), pp. 453–477.

Storper, M., 2018. Separate Worlds? Explaining the current wave of regional economic polarization. *Journal of Economic Geography*, 18(2), pp. 247–270.

Swyngedouw, E., 2009. The antinomies of the postpolitical city: In search of a democratic politics of environmental production. *International Journal of Urban and Regional Research*, 33(3), pp. 601–620.

Zimmermann, K. and Fedeli, V., eds., 2021. *A modern guide to national urban policies in Europe.* Cheltenham, Northampton: Edward Elgar Publishing Limited.

Part I
Political participation

2 Still a red island? Vienna's electoral geography between stability and change

Elisabetta Mocca and Michael Friesenecker

Introduction

The evolution of the policy domains analysed in this book is characterised by the constant presence of the Austrian Social Democratic Party (SPÖ) as the ruling political force in the city council. Moreover, Vienna's social-democratic political monopoly goes even further back in time than the 30 years accounted for in this book. An urban 'red island' floating in 'a black [i.e. conservative] sea' (Öhlinger, 1993, p. 13 in Novy et al., 2009, p. 133), Vienna's municipality has been controlled by the SPÖ since the foundation of the Austrian Republic and its recognition as a federated authority in 1922 – the Nazi period being the only exception. Such a constant feature warrants inclusion in the equation of policy changes that have occurred throughout the three decades considered in this volume.

Although other European capital cities have been governed by social-democratic forces (such as Berlin, Stockholm and particularly Copenhagen), these have not remained in power for almost a century like in Vienna. However, the long-standing social-democratic control of the Austrian capital has not attracted much academic attention, with only a handful of works published, relatively recently, in international scholarly outlets. Research on the topic has analysed Vienna's social-democratic leadership, mainly from an electoral standpoint, focusing on party organisation and the electoral system (Abedi and Siaroff, 1999; Ennser-Jedenastik and Hansen, 2013). To complement these accounts, this chapter explores the relation between Vienna's lasting social-democratic regime and its generous redistributive policy. We rely on *redistribution* as an element of justice (Fraser et al., 2003; Fainstein, 2011), residing at the core of this book, as the analytical lens through which to interpret the Viennese social-democratic dominance. We maintain that, in order to cast light on the Viennese

DOI: 10.4324/9781003133827-3

social-democratic regime, it is necessary not only to examine the SPÖ's territorial organisation and the Austrian electoral arrangements, as previous research has done, but also to factor in the municipal welfare system of social-democratic mould. Vienna's welfare system is characterised by its generous provision across a broad spectrum of services (including social housing, employment policy, utilities, public transport, education and leisure activities; Hatz et al., 2015). By couching the analysis of the policy outputs in the ideological foundations of Vienna's model, this chapter brings policy into conversation with politics.

This approach is operationalised through a multi-phase analysis. First, we map the Austrian parties' national electoral performances to verify whether the *red island* trope still applies (Section "The national elections: a red island in a darkening sea"). Second, we focus on Vienna's electoral landscape by comparing different patterns in national and municipal elections at a sub-municipal level (Section "An increasingly colourful landscape: national and municipal elections in Vienna"). Third, in line with previous research identifying a link between spatial patterns of quality of life and electoral outcomes at national (see Hagerty et al., 2000) and subnational levels (e.g. Lieske, 1990; Ouweneel and Veenhoven, 2016), we analyse the relation between the spatial patterns of municipal elections' outcomes and the aggregated satisfaction of Vienna's residents in relation to socio-economic and environmental conditions and services at the sub-municipal level (Section "The political strength of Vienna's social-democratic regime"). The findings from the analysis are discussed in the concluding section.

The national elections: a red island in a darkening sea

The endurance of the municipal social-democratic government harks back to the early decades of the past century. In the 1920s, Vienna started being portrayed as 'a red island' in the conservative 'black sea' of the rest of the country, to describe the social-democratic 'reformist project of redistribution' (Öhlinger, 1993, p. 13 in Novy et al., 2009, p. 133). This phrase, to some extent, still vividly underscores the divergence between the City's electoral patterns and those of the rest of Austria. Throughout the last 30 years, this trend has become even more pronounced (Table 2.1). In comparison to other federal states and state capitals in Austria, the SPÖ has consistently been the party in Vienna obtaining the majority of the votes in the national elections. The increasing popularity of the right-wing populist Austrian Freedom Party (FPÖ), coupled with a larger consensus gained by the conservative

ÖVP, have shifted the electoral preferences of the other federal states towards the right of the political spectrum since the late 1990s. It has been argued that, at the national level, the *Proporz* system – which foresaw the distribution of political functions, public bodies and social partners between the SPÖ and ÖVP – combined with the consociational architecture of Austrian politics (leading to a *convergence* between the two main parties) fuelled anti-establishment feelings, harnessed by the FPÖ from the 1980s onwards (Art, 2007, p. 334).

Vienna, as a federal state and a municipality, constitutes the most faithful of the SPÖ's stronghold, never switching its political allegiance during the period under consideration, and even beyond (Table 2.1). By way of contrast, the capitals of the other federated states display less continuous party support (except for Eisenstadt for the ÖVP and Linz for the SPÖ), swinging from one of the two main parties, with the FPÖ and the Greens making some gains. Looking at the national electoral results at *Bundesland* level, the national electoral data confirm the image of Vienna as an urban red island amid a sea of Länder whose political preferences at some point swung to (or, always been for) the right of the political spectrum.

Table 2.1 National elections: parties with most votes per federal states and capitals, 1990–2019

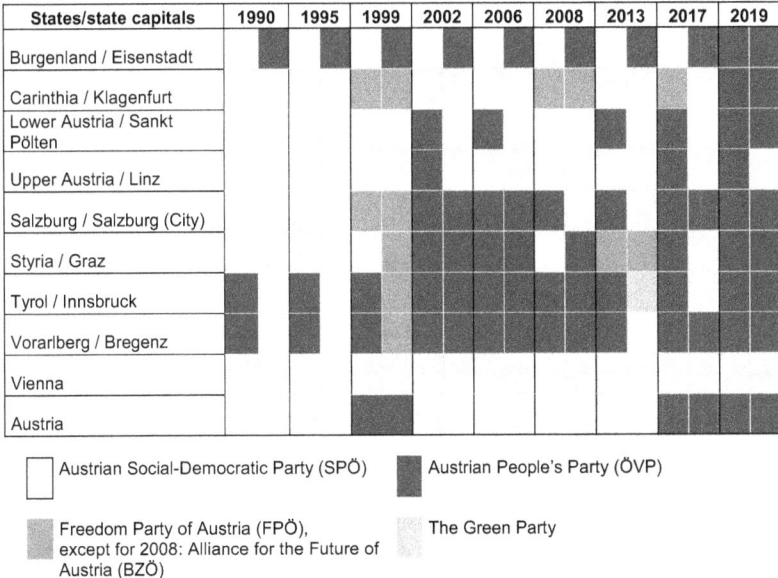

Source: Own calculation based on SORA, 2019, National election results Austria 1919–2017 (OA edition), doi: 10.11587/EQUDAL, AUSSDA Dataverse, V1.

An increasingly colourful landscape: national and municipal elections in Vienna

We now turn to examine Vienna's national and municipal electoral results, unpacking the parties' performance at the district level. The purpose of this analysis is twofold: first, it investigates whether the SPÖ's hegemony has remained uncontested at national and local elections; second, the focus on the local elections lays the groundwork for the correlation analysis performed next. Since Vienna is both a municipality and a *Bundesland*, municipal elections are the same as the *Länder* elections, and function as elections to the city council.

Austria's territorial variations in electoral patterns have been observed by some international electoral research. Abedi and Siaroff (1999) reported on how *Länder* and national election results showed divergent trends in the 1983–1997 period, identifying the driver of this rift in the ÖVP's localised party structure, which conferred its greater electoral success in the *Länder* elections. The authors found that the SPÖ's electoral patterns in Vienna did not reflect an increasing divide between *Länder* and national elections, but rather displayed similar voting performances at both levels (ibid.). On the contrary, Ennser-Jedenastik and Hansen (2013, p. 787), who study the nationalisation of Austrian party systems, suggest that 'the most nationalised party system is found in Vienna', as cities have always been the social-democratic bulwarks in Austria.

Our analysis shows that the synchronous voting pattern reported by Abedi and Siaroff (1999) for Vienna at the city level until the 1990s shifted at beginning of the millennium (Figure 2.1). By breaking the development of the national electoral results down by district level and comparing it to the municipal electoral results, the picture confirms a diverging, but also changing, pattern between national and local elections. In the 1990s, the overwhelming majority of districts voted for the SPÖ in the national elections, with some leaning towards the ÖVP, although the vote shares for the SPÖ decreased over time in almost every district (Figure 2.1). The 2000s witnessed the entrance of the Greens in the national political arena. Since the 2002 national elections, the Greens gained growing consensus in the wealthier inner districts. Such progressive growth was halted in 2017, when the Greens were wiped out from Vienna's electoral map due to a party split at the national level. Voters in the *green* districts then mostly returned to the SPÖ. However, the Greens made a successful comeback in the 2019 national election, forming a coalition with the ÖVP at the federal level. The Greens' electoral triumph is reflected in the electoral map

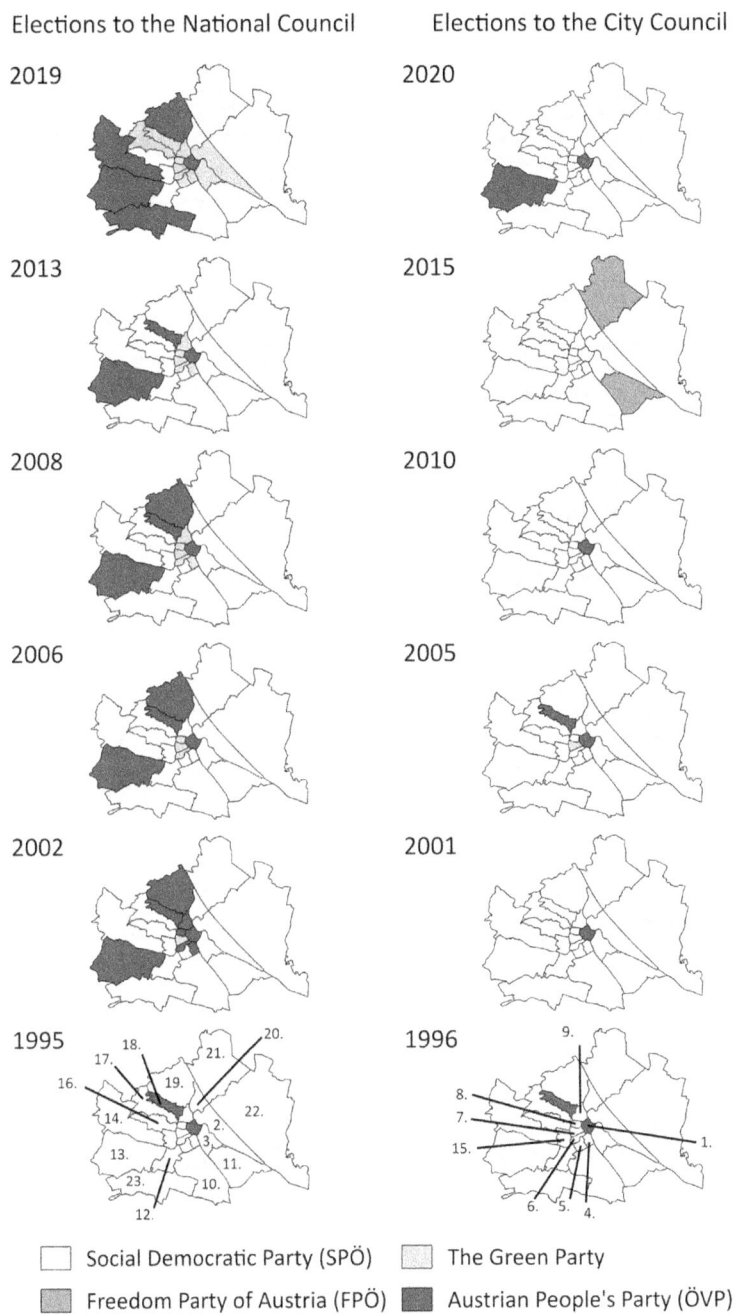

Figure 2.1 Comparison of national and municipal elections: parties with most votes per districts, 1995–2020.

Source: Data.gv.at CC BY 4.0, Statistical Yearbooks of Vienna, BMI – https://bit.ly/3tOCNTf, Author's own elaboration.

of Vienna, where the party gained a majority of votes in 10 out of 23 districts, especially in the inner districts. This changing electoral outcome appears to be related to an increasing re-urbanisation of inner-city districts by new urban middle classes and a slightly stronger effect of socio-economic features in explaining socio-spatial segregation (Hatz et al., 2015). However, the same election also saw the ÖVP gaining the majority of votes in the outer, wealthier districts and in the first district (an ÖVP bulwark for the time frame considered).

The national elections witnessed a weakening of the red island metaphor in the new millennium. Meanwhile, the data show that this trope has held up for the city council elections, with the SPÖ gaining the overwhelming majority of the districts over the timespan considered. However, other parties, primarily the ÖVP but also the Greens and, more recently, the FPÖ, made limited inroads in the municipal electoral competition.

From 1991 to 2001, the ÖVP constituted the only opponent of the SPÖ in very few districts (Figure 2.1). The first district is strongly conservative, with the ÖVP being the most voted-for party in all of the elections considered in our study – except for the 2015 municipal elections, when the SPÖ took the most votes in this district. In 1996, the change of the Viennese SPÖ's leadership (Michael Häupl replaced Helmut Zilk) led to the party's lowest historic result, forcing it to form a coalition with the ÖVP. In 2001, the SPÖ regained full control of the city council with no coalition partner.

While not gaining the majority of the votes in any Viennese district, the FPÖ fared well in the 1991 municipal elections, when it obtained 22.5% of the votes, 'more than doubling its total from 1987 and robbing the SPÖ of the absolute majority it had enjoyed since 1954' (Art, 2007, pp. 343–344). More importantly, the 2015 elections saw the FPÖ conquering the 11th and 21st districts – working-class areas with a high density of social housing. This pattern seems to be associated with an increasing residualisation of low-status groups in municipal housing estates (Hatz et al., 2015). In 2015, the FPÖ received nearly one-third of the votes (30.79%), their highest share of the votes ever obtained in Vienna. Therefore, since the 1990s, the FPÖ has acquired growing political weight in the city council. However, the national scandal of the FPÖ, the so-called Ibiza affair in 2019, which also led to a local party split, massively weakened the FPÖ's influence in the 2020 elections. Indeed, FPÖ votes dropped from around 30% to 7%, with many voters either returning to the SPÖ or abstaining.

The Greens appeared to be a less challenging opponent for the SPÖ at the municipal level, as their vote shares in the inner-city districts are lower than in the national elections. This suggests that potential Greens' voters make a clear distinction between national and local policies. In Vienna's electoral map, the Greens only appeared in 2005 when they gained the majority of votes in the 7th district – which displays higher concentrations of young, well-educated urban professionals and creatives – then quickly disappeared again in the next elections (Figure 2.1). While the Greens' political relevance should not be understated, being the junior partner in two coalitions with the SPÖ from 2010 to 2020, their shares of the votes in municipal elections are, on average, fairly modest when compared to those gained in the national elections.

The data show that Viennese voters tend to vote differently in the national and municipal elections. While not rejecting the validity of previous research considering the voting system and party organisation as factors that favoured the SPÖ's control of Vienna, we analyse the century-long city's allegiance to the SPÖ at the municipal level in relation to local social policies implemented by the latter. In the next section, we probe this relationship.

The political strength of Vienna's social-democratic regime

The key role of the municipality in service delivery harks back to the second decade of the 19th century. In particular, since 1919, under the leadership of Reumann (the first social-democratic mayor) and especially after becoming a *Bundesland* in 1922, the city embraced an extensive programme of reform that was of municipal social-democratic bent, entailing municipal control and provision of goods and services, such as housing, welfare, healthcare, education and culture (Graicer, 1989; Kadi and Suitner, 2019). As documented in the other chapters in this volume, the City's policies were adapted to socio-economic and institutional changes, such as population growth, socio-demographic changes and EU membership. While part of the early social-democratic legacy is still entrenched in the City's generous system of public service provision, today's ideological posture in Vienna has moved away from the original municipal socialist stance in favour of a mild neoliberal policy style (Novy and Hammer, 2007). Notably, Vienna's inclusive social housing approach has been impacted by a recommodification of some housing segments, which has compounded the social and spatial divide (Hatz et al., 2015; Kadi, 2015, see Chapter 4 by Litschauer and Friesenecker in this volume). Similarly, in recent decades, social disparity has increasingly affected the Viennese labour market (Chapter 7 by Riederer et al. in this volume).

To explore the relationship between patterns of satisfaction with socio-economic and environmental conditions, the City's service provision and voting patterns, we undertook a correlation analysis at district level. Additionally, we checked for potential correlations between spatial patterns of voter turnout and satisfaction to shed light on the possible role of protest votes. We employed data drawn from (i) the *Viennese Quality of Life Survey* (VQLS), and (ii) the city council elections. While the first of these sources accounts for the spatial pattern in the aggregated residents' degree of satisfaction with the City's services, socio-economic conditions and living environment per district, the latter provided area-based data on each of the main parties' electoral performance since 1996.[1] Due to data constraints, we selected data from the elections that were as close as possible to those of the VQLS (elections: 1996, 2005, 2010, 2015 and 2020; VQLS: 1995, 2003, 2008, 2013 and 2018). The VQLS, with a sample size of around 8,000 respondents, is representative of the populations of the Viennese districts. Unfortunately, as the VQLS does not provide individualised electoral indicators, we combined this database with area-based national and municipal electoral data. In light of the perils of the 'ecological fallacy' lurking in those analyses 'drawing inferences about individual behaviour from aggregate data' (Kramer, 1983, p. 92), we avoid interpreting individual relationships between satisfaction and voting behaviour and focus on relations between spatial patterns of electoral outcomes and satisfaction levels.

The data indicate a significant positive correlation between the composite satisfaction indicator and voter turnout (Table 2.2). This result suggests that areas displaying higher life satisfaction are more likely to vote in the municipal elections, whereas areas characterised by lower satisfaction show less political participation in local elections. To refine our analysis, we run a correlation between satisfaction for different socio-economic and urban aspects and parties' share of the votes.

From 2010 onwards, the results for the SPÖ indicate that those districts where people are, on average, more satisfied show lower probabilities for high SPÖ votes in the city council elections (despite both the SPÖ's vote shares and life quality satisfaction always remaining fairly high). In particular, the analysis of the individual policy domains of the composite indicator suggests that the lower the perceived quality of the neighbourhood and cultural offer in a district, the lower the SPÖ's share of the vote for the entire period tends to be. Since 2010, low levels of satisfaction with the housing situation and, since 2015, the household financial situation have been related to levels of SPÖ votes. Satisfaction with environmental quality and occupational conditions recently seems to have become less important in relation to spatial patterns of sub-municipal SPÖ strongholds.

As for the FPÖ, the results show a significant negative correlation between the district's vote share and satisfaction with the neighbourhood and cultural offer. More markedly in the last election, the correlation results appear to be broadly similar to those displayed by the SPÖ: our findings indicate a negative correlation between the FPÖ's share of the votes and levels of satisfaction for a series of indicators, such as household financial conditions, occupation, housing, transport, health system and administration.

Moving to the ÖVP, the data show a statistically significant positive correlation, especially between ÖVP's vote share and the district's levels of satisfaction for the neighbourhood and also cultural offer, although almost no significant correlations could be measured for 2020. Additionally, for some of the years under analysis, there is a positive correlation between the ÖVP's share of the votes and housing situation, environmental quality, household financial situation and occupation. To some extent, the correlation results for the ÖVP's vote share and life satisfaction appear to mirror opposite circumstances to that of the SPÖ. This may point at the different electoral base of the two parties, with the ÖVP more likely to attract well-off voters.

Regarding the Greens, besides a negative correlation between the district's vote shares and lower levels of satisfaction with local kindergartens, the data for the last election point at a positive significant correlation with the composite satisfaction indicator. Indeed, the share of Greens' votes positively correlates with districts that show higher satisfaction with the neighbourhood, public transport, health systems, occupation and the administration. With regard to Neos, a liberal party founded in 2012 (Ennser-Jedenastik and Bodlos, 2019), the highly significant positive correlation of the last two elections relate predominantly to districts with higher levels of satisfaction from many aspects, especially the neighbourhood, the housing situation and the financial position of the household.

To better interpret the correlation results, we examined the relationship between the parties' vote shares and life satisfaction by district. An interesting finding is the correlation results for those districts lying below Vienna's average net-income, such as the 10th, 11th and 20th districts (Stadt Wien, 2020, p. 150). These districts display higher probabilities of voting for the SPÖ (Figure 2.2). These very same areas also appear to have higher vote shares for the FPÖ, hinting at how the latter may erode the electoral base of the Social Democratic Party. It is worth noting that the 20th district has recently become one of the

Table 2.2 Correlation of vote shares for elections to district councils and satisfaction per district (N=23)

Satisfaction with…	SPÖ						ÖVP						FPÖ					
	1996	2005	2010	2015	2020		1996	2005	2010	2015	2020		1996	2005	2010	2015	2020	
Composite satisfaction indicator	−0.162	−0.020	−.486**	−.470**	−.578**		0.257	0.154	.573**	.439**	0.241		−.296*	−0.043	−0.233	−0.209	−.557**	
…neighbourhood	n.a.	−.415**	−.581**	−.581**	−.594**		n.a.	.549**	.573**	.518**	0.225		n.a.	−.407**	−.360*	−.320*	−.510**	
…housing situation	−0.194	−0.107	−.439**	−.565**	−.436**		.304*	0.289	.478**	.549**	0.273		−.344*	−0.099	−0.154	−0.209	−.399**	
…schools	n.a	0.091	−.423**	−0.174	−0.131		n.a	−0.067	.415**	0.143	−0.127		n.a	0.099	−0.265	0.040	−0.261	
…kindergartens	n.a.	.320*	.383**	0.020	−0.063		n.a.	−0.265	−.296*	−0.130	0.170		n.a.	0.281	.447**	.360*	−0.028	
…cultural offer	n.a.	−.352*	−.573**	−.352*	−.349*		n.a.	.296*	.549**	.320*	.296*		n.a.	−.312*	−.510**	−.360*	−0.233	
…environmental quality	n.a.	−0.028	−0.304	−0.383*	−0.293		n.a.	0.146	0.281	.431**	.399**		n.a.	−0.004	−0.209	−0.186	−0.146	
…public transport	n.a.	−0.063	−0.198	0.083	−.372*		n.a.	−0.040	0.158	0.123	−0.083		n.a.	−0.024	−.372*	−0.289	−.534**	
…financial situation of household	n.a.	0.043	−0.233	−.502**	−.491**		n.a.	0.170	0.273	.423**	.304*		n.a.	0.036	−0.012	−0.194	−.336*	
…salary	−0.099	−0.075	−0.202	0.091	−0.230		0.209	0.130	0.289	−0.075	0.186		−0.217	−0.099	−0.059	0.099	−0.059	
…occupation	n.a.	−0.119	−.415**	−.312*	−0.293		n.a.	.301*	.439**	0.281	−0.051		n.a.	−0.095	−0.241	−0.178	−.423**	
…job	−0.123	−0.051	−.431**	−0.111	−0.099		0.233	0.123	.455**	0.079	0.048		−0.289	−0.123	−0.225	−0.048	−0.016	
…health system	n.a.	−.182**	−0.036	−0.265	−.377*		n.a.	0.174	0.091	0.202	0.000		n.a.	−0.174	0.075	0.178	−.475**	
…administration	n.a.	.391**	−0.080	−0.170	−0.364*		n.a.	−0.257	0.111	0.154	−0.028		n.a.	.352*	0.048	0.083	−.494**	

Satisfaction with…	Greens					Neos		Turnout				
	1996	2005	2010	2015	2020	2015	2020	1996	2005	2010	2015	2020
Composite satisfaction indicator	−0.138	−0.170	0.067	0.043	.431**	.510**	.597**	.478**	.455**	.565**	.605**	.597**
…neighbourhood	n.a	0.162	0.209	0.138	.399**	.573**	.597**		.723**	.708**	.684**	.723**
…housing situation	−0.091	−0.130	0.036	0.043	.320*	.494**	.423**	.431**	.715**	.565**	.668**	.534**
…schools	n.a	−0.091	0.146	−0.158	.309*	0.166	0.135		−0.036	.344*	0.111	0.246
…kindergartens	n.a	−.336*	−.470**	−.320*	−0.020	−0.186	0.099		−0.012	−0.209	−0.043	0.083
…cultural offer	n.a	0.225	.344*	0.273	0.202	.407**	.383*		.328*	.415**	.613**	.383*
…environmental quality	n.a	−0.130	0.075	0.099	0.020	.391**	.328*		.320*	.383*	.486**	0.233
…public transport	n.a	0.143	.483**	0.249	.502**	0.209	.368*		−0.214	−0.087	0.051	.415**
…financial situation of household	n.a	−0.217	−0.075	0.028	0.289	.431**	.502**		.407**	.423**	.652**	.455**
…salary	−0.170	−0.004	−0.091	−0.138	−0.036	−0.083	0.178	.494**	.368*	0.202	0.043	0.146
…occupation	n.a	−0.071	0.154	0.028	.486**	.304*	0.241		.404**	.557**	.415**	.352*
…job	−0.083	−0.028	0.123	−0.071	0.032	0.119	0.071	.375*	0.217	.447**	0.071	0.008
…health system	n.a	0.087	−0.209	0.091	.444**	0.241	.356*		0.190	−0.043	0.194	.420**
…administration	n.a	−.455**	−0.111	−0.004	.462**	0.178	0.344		0.1541	0.223	0.225	.344

Sources: VQLS 1995, 2003, 2008, 2013, 2018 for satisfaction data; data.gv.at, Statistical Yearbooks of the Vienna, BMI for voting data.
+Based on Kendall's tau-b correlation coefficient.
*The correlation is significant at the level of 0.05 (two-sided).
**The correlation is significant at the level of 0.01 (two-sided).

most diverse in Vienna, where slightly over 50% of residents have a migration background and 23.8% of the population do not have the right to vote in any elections; similarly, the 10th and 11th districts are comprised of a sizeable portion of non-native residents, among which 23.4% and 18%, respectively, cannot vote in any elections.[2] Further, these three districts seem to be less likely to vote for the ÖVP, Greens and Neos. The district-level results appear to confirm the existence of a spatial relationship between high levels of life satisfaction and

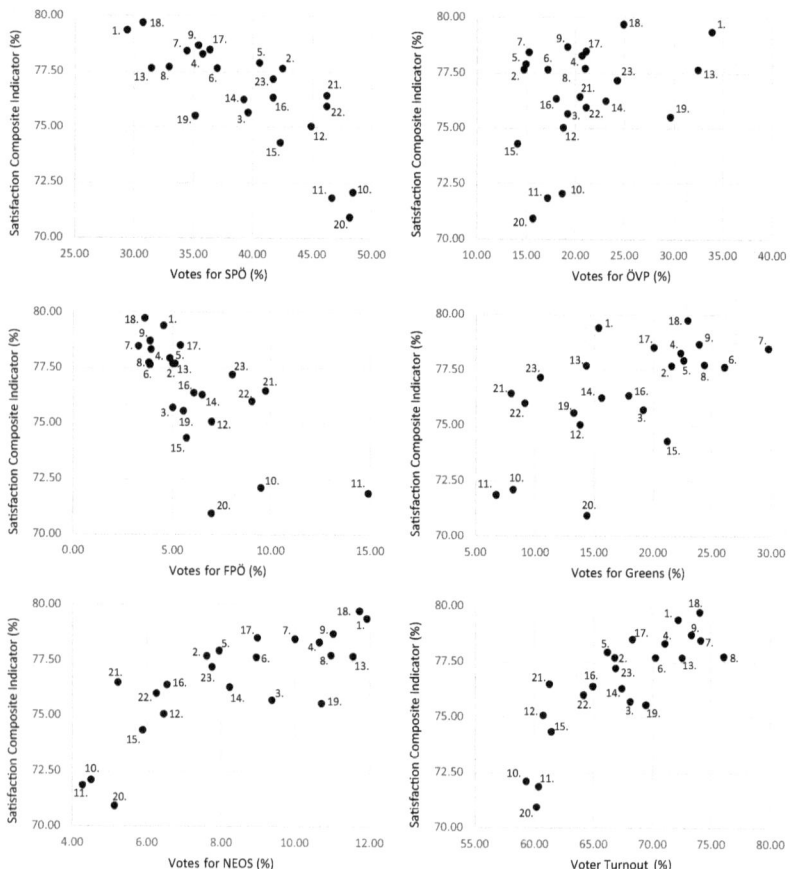

Figure 2.2 Scatter plot for vote shares (2020) and satisfaction composite indicator (2018).

Source: MA62 Stadt Wien, Viennese Life Quality Survey 2018, Author's own elaboration.

the probability of voting for Greens and Neos. Overall, these findings indicate that the increasing influence of social-spatial disparities in income inequality suggested by the correlation analysis (such as lower levels of satisfaction with one's housing situation, neighbourhood and financial situation), relate to specific electoral outcomes at the district level.

Two complementary explanations might justify the correlation results. First, the findings appear to suggest that the Red Vienna myth has (at least partly) lost its ideological grip in some Viennese districts: while electoral performance confirms the SPÖ as the undisputed ruler of the City, its traditional redistributive social policy repertoire may not be sufficient to achieve a significant number of votes in those areas with a higher concentration of more affluent residents than in those areas with less affluent residents. Second, the correlation results hint that those areas where, on average, Viennese residents are less satisfied with their general living conditions have higher SPÖ vote shares. A cautious interpretation may convey the impression that the SPÖ is still conceptualised by its voters as a service provider, in line with its traditional mission. However, further research would be needed to cast further light on the link between service supply and voting patterns at an individual level.

Conclusions

This chapter mapped the persistence of the SPÖ in Vienna in the national and municipal elections over the last 30 years. Seeking to go beyond explanations hinging on party system organisation, we linked the analysis of the SPÖ's electoral success in Vienna to the redistributive municipal welfare system built over a century. Therefore, we framed our investigation by employing the concept of redistribution, which helped us to understand how redistributive policies still constitute a terrain where parties compete for votes.

The data points out how the red island trope still describes the political identity of the Austrian capital. While the political preferences of most Austrian federal states' capitals swung since the late 1990s, the SPÖ was able to retain its control of Vienna. This contrasts with other European capital cities, such as Stockholm or London, which have undergone political change in the last decades. As the findings show, the diverging spatial patterns of voting outcomes between the national and municipal elections support the argument that Vienna has been successful in keeping its reputation as a just, social-democratic city thanks to its local redistributive policies. While the SPÖ received the majority of the votes for the National Council elections in almost all Viennese districts until the 2002 election, this spatial dominance was progressively weakened, as the ÖVP and the Greens increased their share of votes in more and more districts over the years. However, regarding the municipal elections, the SPÖ has been able to retain its power, with very few districts voting for the ÖVP and the FPÖ. This marked contrast to the outcomes at the national level seems to suggest residents' endorsement of the social-democrats' local redistributive policies.

Nevertheless, our correlation analysis of municipal elections at the district level revealed that socio-economic and spatial divides are eroding the SPÖ's electoral base, possibly fuelling protest votes, as indicated by higher FPÖ shares and lower turnout rates in areas with low satisfaction. These findings resonate with results from opinion polls of the 2020 municipal elections, where a majority of FPÖ voters indicated that they perceived of Vienna as being run-down and of losing its quality of life (Sora, 2020). As FPÖ voters in the 2020 municipal elections tended to be young, blue-collar workers (Sora, 2020), Vienna's redistributive policies may not have been fully able to cater for some of its least-well off population. Thus, the FPÖ capitalises on such discontent, attracting the SPÖ's traditional working-class electoral base, which is especially evident in the southern and northeastern outskirts of Vienna. On the contrary, according to Sora's opinion poll (2020), SPÖ voters appear to see Vienna as a city worth living in. Our analysis suggests that this is related to areas that, on average, show lower satisfaction with the quality of the neighbourhoods, housing and financial situation, since these areas negatively correlate with the share of SPÖ's votes. This finding conveys the impression that, at the local level, the SPÖ is mainly conceived of as a front-line service provider, possibly implying a positive public perception with regard to its ability to design effective policies to address problematic living conditions.

In general, the evidence showed that districts with higher levels of life satisfaction negatively correlate with the SPÖ and FPÖ vote shares at municipal elections. Our analysis appears to hint that the SPÖ may fall short of capturing the requests from the better-off sectors of the local population, which have partly turned to the ÖVP, Greens and Neos. This finding may indicate incipient (yet not decisive) signs of new political cleavages, rendered in the literature by Inglehart's materialism/postmaterialism dichotomy, Kriesi and colleagues' 'winners and losers of globalisation' argument and Hooghe and Marks' 'Green-Alternative-Liberal and Traditional-Authoritarian-Nationalist' divide

(Ford and Jennings, 2020, p. 298). These authors submit how emerging political cleavages see contemporary Western society as being split along the lines of highly educated, highly skilled and mobile class individuals and less qualified, less mobile and more traditional individuals (ibid.).

Ultimately, this chapter showed that the scope and generosity of local redistributive policies may act as a pull attracting voters. This indicates that Vienna's social-democratic control and its reputation as a *just city* may depend upon the SPÖ's ability to address contemporary socio-economic and ecological challenges, while preserving its deep-seated redistributive policy approach.

Notes

1 The choice of this year as the first temporal point is due to the fact that 1995 is the first year with available data from the life satisfaction survey and 1996 is the closest electoral year.
2 https://bit.ly/3tOUAtK

References

Abedi, A. and Siaroff, A., 1999. The mirror has broken: Increasing divergence between national and Land elections in Austria. *German Politics*, 8(1), pp. 207–227.

Art, D., 2007. Reacting to the radical right: Lessons from Germany and Austria. *Party Politics*, 13(3), pp. 331–349.

Ennser-Jedenastik, L. and Bodlos, A., 2019. Liberal parties in Austria. In: Van Haute, E. and Close, C., eds., 2019. *Liberal parties in Europe*. London and New York: Routledge, pp. 129–145.

Ennser-Jedenastik, L., and Hansen, M.E., 2013. The contingent nature of local party system nationalisation: The case of Austria 1985–2009. *Local Government Studies*, 39(6), pp. 777–791.

Fainstein, S.S., 2011. *The just city*. Ithaca, NY: Cornell University Press.

Ford, R. and Jennings, W., 2020. The changing cleavage politics of Western Europe. *Annual Review of Political Science*, 23(1), pp. 295–314.

Fraser, N., Honneth, A., Golb, J., Imgram, J. and Wilke, C., 2003. *Redistribution or recognition?: A political-philosophical Exchange*. London: Verso.

Graicer, I., 1989. Red Vienna and municipal socialism in Tel Aviv 1925–1928. *Journal of Historical Geography*, 15(4), pp. 385–401.

Hagerty, M.R., Naik, P. and Tsai, C.-L., 2000. The effects of quality of life on national elections: A multi-country analysis. *Social Indicators Research*, 49(3), pp. 347–362.

Hatz, G., Kohlbacher, J. and Reeger, U., 2015. Socio-economic segregation in Vienna: A social-oriented approach to urban planning and housing. In:

Tammaru, T., Van Ham, M., Marcińczak, S. and Musterd, S., eds., 2015. *Socio-economic segregation in European capital cities. East meets west*. London and New York: Routledge, pp. 80–109.

Kadi, J., 2015. Recommodifying housing in formerly "Red" Vienna? *Housing, Theory, and Society*, 32(3), pp. 247–65.

Kadi, J. and Suitner, J., 2019. Red Vienna, 1919–1934. In: Orum, A.M., ed., 2019. *The Wiley Blackwell encyclopedia of urban and regional studies*. Wiley Blackwell, pp. 1–5.

Kramer, G.H., 1983. The ecological fallacy revisited: Aggregate-versus individual-level findings on economics and elections, and sociotropic voting. *The American Political Science Review*, 77(1), pp. 92–111.

Lieske, J. 1990. The correlates of life quality in U.S. metropolitan areas. *Publius*, 20(1), pp. 43–54.

Novy, A., and Hammer, E., 2007. Radical innovation in the era of liberal governance: The case of Vienna. *European Urban and Regional Studies*, 14(3), pp. 210–222.

Novy, A., Hammer, E. and Leubolt, B., 2009. Social innovation and governance of scale in Austria. In: MacCallum, D., Moulaert, F., Hillier, J. and Vicari Haddock, S., eds., 2009. *Social innovation and territorial development*. Surrey: Ashgate Publishing, pp. 131–148.

Öhlinger, W., 1993. *Das Rote Wien, 1918–1934: Historisches Museum der Stadt Wien, 17.6.-5.9. 1993*. Vol. 177. Eigenverlag der Museen der Stadt Wien.

Ouweneel, P. and Veenhoven, R., 2016. Happy protest voters: The case of Rotterdam 1997–2009. *Social Indicators Research*, 126(2), pp. 739–756.

Sora. 2020. *Vienna City council elections 2020*. [online] Available at: https://bit.ly/3hx6O7C [Accessed 17 May 2021].

Stadt Wien. 2020. *Statistisches Jahrbuch der Stadt Wien 2020*. [pdf] Available at: https://bit.ly/3btivsc [Accessed 17 May 2021].

3 Unlocking the door of the city hall

Vienna's participatory shift in urban development policy

Byeongsun Ahn and Elisabetta Mocca

Introduction

Participation is the holy grail of recent policy-making and has drawn significant academic attention. Indeed, progressive policy-makers, as well as political scholars, seem to agree upon the need to involve citizens in public affairs to expand democracy. However, as Arnstein (1969) already noted in the late 1960s, there may be different degrees of participation, from tokenism to citizen power. In practice, the top-down form of participation commonly allowed by public actors may or may not consist of emancipatory mechanisms that enable a mutual partnership between citizens and powerholders in decision-making and policy design.

In recent years, urban researchers have thrown light on participatory mechanisms rolled out in various cities across the world, ranging from Latin America (Goldfrank, 2007) to the United States and the United Kingdom (Elwood, 2004), and from continental Europe (Garcia, 2006) to China (Zhang et al., 2020). Among them, citizen participation in Vienna has been studied vis-à-vis communitarian urban development policies (for its historical evolution, see Suitner, 2020). Extant research has noted how participatory policies have been implemented in a context dominated by the long-lasting legacy of a vertical policy-making style harking back to Red Vienna and consolidated in the post-war period (Novy and Hammer, 2007). Notwithstanding some changes in the political landscape in recent years (for the erosion of the Social-Democrats' electoral base, see Chapter 2 by Mocca and Friesenecker in this volume), the City of Vienna has often been described as a 'Weberian-style administration' (Kornberger, et al., 2017, p. 180), characterised by a 'corporatist' (Novy et al., 2001, p. 131), 'top-down' (Novy and Hammer, 2007, p. 213) governing system. Moreover, it has been observed that endeavours to make Viennese policy-making more inclusive have been hindered by looming clientelism (Dangeschat and Hamedinger, 2009).

Consequently, non-tokenistic involvement of citizens in decision-making appears to find little room in the Viennese policy-making and deliberative process. In effect, much of the decision-making in urban development has often been centrally designed and implemented, with little delegated power to non-public actors for community control. Nevertheless, following international trends towards greater involvement of citizens in public affairs, some inroads into Vienna's interventionist and vertical policy approach have been made. Since the 1970s, the city government gradually introduced mechanisms to draw citizens into policy design and deliberation, especially in small-scale planning. Whilst such citizen involvement has been expanded through the development of the *Vienna Model* over the decades that followed, some obstacles to full representation of local interests in non-electoral participation still persist, as discussed in the ensuing sections.

This chapter highlights the political dimension of urban justice in Vienna, which cannot be reduced to resource maldistribution or misrecognition of residents' status – examined elsewhere in this volume. Therefore, the analysis presented here builds on Fraser's three-dimensional theory of justice, 'incorporating the political dimension of representation, alongside the economic dimension of distribution and the cultural dimension of recognition' (Fraser, 2010, p. 15). The extent of representation, as a precondition for the other two dimensions of distribution and recognition (for access to labour welfare, see Chapter 6 by Ahn and Kazepov; for access to housing, see Chapter 4 by Litschauer and Friesenecker), entails strong power implications. In this regard, the degree to which public actors open the policy-making process up to civil society, including less privileged residents, determines the policy outcomes. Therefore, the historical trajectory of Vienna's participatory mechanisms begs the question as to how this particular path has developed over time, which social groups benefit from this path, and which policy instruments have been deployed to foster or prevent the mainstreaming of citizen participation in the City's policy-making process.

The historical pathway towards the Vienna Model

Prompted by the suburbanisation of the inner-city districts, a new planning paradigm emerged in Vienna in the 1970s. The City moved away from the functionalist planning model of the previous decade, which had focused on car-centric urban expansion (Feuerstein and

Fitz, 2009). In this new era, the city government set the renewal of the dilapidated inner-city districts (between the outer ring-road and the 1st district) as a key task, where poor quality residential buildings required refurbishment interventions. A shift also emerged in response to growing public opposition to some of the large-scale development projects that were initiated throughout this period. The latter led to the demolition of the city's historical landmarks, such as Florianikirche (1965) and the Otto-Wagner Pavilion in the 12th district (1969), to make room for high-rise- and highway constructions in the central areas of the city. Between the late 1960s and the early 1970s, bottom-up initiatives against the functionalist urban projects, such as a new residential construction in a former red-light quarter (*Spittelberg*) in the seventh district, sparked debates on the restructuring of the City's planning system. The lack of citizen participation prior to that point in the planning process and the absence of an effective management structure in urban development were problematised within such discussions (Feuerstein and Fitz, 2009). In response, the city government began to deploy new participatory instruments to broaden resident involvement in urban renewal projects, where tenants and property owners became incorporated into the planning process. Subsequently, the institutionalisation of participatory planning then came about, building upon the legal amendments that followed this participatory turn, for example, the Vienna Building Code, the Old City Protection Act in 1972, and the Urban Renewal Act in 1974. This aimed not only to make locally specific problems more accessible to the planning authorities but also to reverse the declining public trust in the City's urban development strategies (Berger, 1984). Such changes laid the foundations for the City's new planning system where, on the one hand, active participation and engagement curbed potential conflicts between different residential groups. On the other hand, it provided a strong regulatory framework – complementing its housing policy – and mitigated negative spillovers of housing and urban development (for the recent development of Vienna's housing and tenancy regulatory system, see Chapter 4 by Litschauer and Friesenecker).

At the same time, a momentum for greater citizen participation initiated a process of innovation in the City's planning management approach, which introduced a new collaborative arrangement in large-scale development projects. Contrary to the expert-led technocratic approaches in the previous planning model, the new mode of governance enabled deliberation and the participation of a diverse range of both institutional and non-institutional actors, mediated by a decentralised control office. This method, referred to as the 'Vienna Model'

(Freisitzer and Maurer, 1985), formalised an institutional space for public-private-citizen partnership, based on horizontal cooperation between planning groups and public administration. Whilst citizens' participation mainly still occurred in the form of information dissemination in the planning process, reforms in the late 1980s began to adopt an entrepreneurial approach to urban development. Market elements, such as competitive tendering, were incorporated into the City's new planning paradigm. In contrast to the 1980s' New Public Management reforms in the Anglo-American sphere, however, the rescaling process in Vienna retained a corporative network with a strong level of interdependency, beyond strictly contractual relations between institutional and non-institutional actors. This differed greatly from, for example, the urban policies adopted during the same period in Labour-led British cities, such as Barnsley, Rotherham and Liverpool, whose leaders began to embrace market-led regeneration in response to the defeat of the miners' strike in the mid-1980s, economic decline in working-class areas, and growing support for Thatcher's central government in their constituencies (Davies, 2004). Similarly, in light of shrinking federal public expenditure, from the late 1970s onwards (especially during Reagan's administration), American cities relied on the taxation of private businesses located in their areas to subsidise urban regeneration (Teaford, 2000). Unlike these examples, a strong presence of zoning and land-use regulations in Vienna mitigated the dominance of private market actors, whose participation in urban development was – and still is – controlled by a socially oriented selection procedure, involving all relevant municipal departments (see Chapter 4 by Litschauer and Friesenecker).

The restructuring of the planning system was simultaneously accompanied by the decentralisation of the city administration and the expansion of direct democracy. After a redevelopment plan of a large green space (*Sternwartepark*) was rejected in the first-ever city-level opinion poll in 1973, a number of reforms enhancing direct democracy were introduced under the newly nominated Social-Democratic (SPÖ) mayor, Leopold Gratz. Further, the SPÖ-led city council institutionalised different instruments of direct democracy, although the extent of citizens' influence in municipal policy-making was limited by its non-binding nature, as well as restrictive quorum and turnout rules (Pleschberger and Mertens, 2012). As a result, direct democracy in Vienna mainly occurred as an outcome of inter-party competition within the city council, employed to either approve or object to urban development proposals by the Social-Democrats in power or their opposition, the Christian-Democrats (ÖVP). Direct democracy equated to the use of opinion poll (*Volksbefragung*), mostly employed as a means of seeking popular support for policy implementation. However, its non-binding nature allowed political parties to pursue their urban development plans regardless of the outcome. This was true especially in the 1980s, as in the case of the *Austria Centre Vienna*[1] (1981), which were subject to criticism by opposition parties and citizens' initiatives (Pleschberger and Mertens, 2012). With the decentralisation process in the late 1980s, a new mode of direct citizen participation was introduced at the district level, which expanded the right of codetermination of the local population within the districts' sphere of competence. Notwithstanding the expansion of participatory platforms, especially for non-institutional experts, the extent of direct citizen participation in this period was still dominated by tokenistic involvement in large-scale urban development, mostly occurring in the form of information dissemination. Emerging participatory opportunities tended to be delegated to decentralised institutions, such as the Urban Renewal Offices (since 1974), often as an ad hoc reaction to grassroots discontent (e.g. *Planquadrate*, 1974–1979). Such bodies were not endowed with sufficient institutional competence and financial autonomy (Förster, 1988). In the years that followed, a more communitarian approach to direct citizen participation began to be incrementally incorporated. As we will see, however, the field and reach of its application remained constrained.

New approaches to participation starting from the 1990s

A new phase of participatory urban governance began in the early 1990s, as emerging urban challenges necessitated a reorientation of the planning strategies set in the previous decade. In light of the growing demand for economic competitiveness, place-branding strategies came to the fore in the City's urban policy priorities (Mayerhofer and Wolfmayr-Schnitzer, 1996). This shift occurred whilst maintaining the core concept of the Vienna Model: a mix of urban renewal and expansion strategies incorporated economic growth as one of the major policy objectives to enhance its cultural, technological, and economic attractiveness in the growing competition between cities (Mattl, 2000). One such example was the EXPO-Project, which was planned to expand the United Nations complex into an international congress quarter and develop a new urban centre near the Danube after a twin-city World's Fair with Budapest in 1995. As public worries grew concerning real estate speculation, tax burden and other issues, the right-wing Freedom Party (FPÖ) started a referendum petition in opposition to the twin-city World's Fair (Schimak, 1993). In response, an opinion poll was launched in 1991 by the SPÖ and the ÖVP, who were looking for popular support for the project, though it was ultimately rejected by the voters. This political failure of the two major parties marked the beginning of a phase of reorganisation in the participatory tools in urban planning. In contrast to outcome-oriented, one-way consultations, there arose a need to sustain public engagement in small-scale urban development, by which the local population could be incorporated into the entire planning process through a diverse range of participatory opportunities (Antalovsky and König, 1994). Accordingly, smaller working groups, consisting of public institutions, experts and residents, were formed through localised planning projects, where strategic planning concepts could be co-produced following multiple rounds of extensive information gathering and public discussions. This was accompanied by the further restructuring of the city

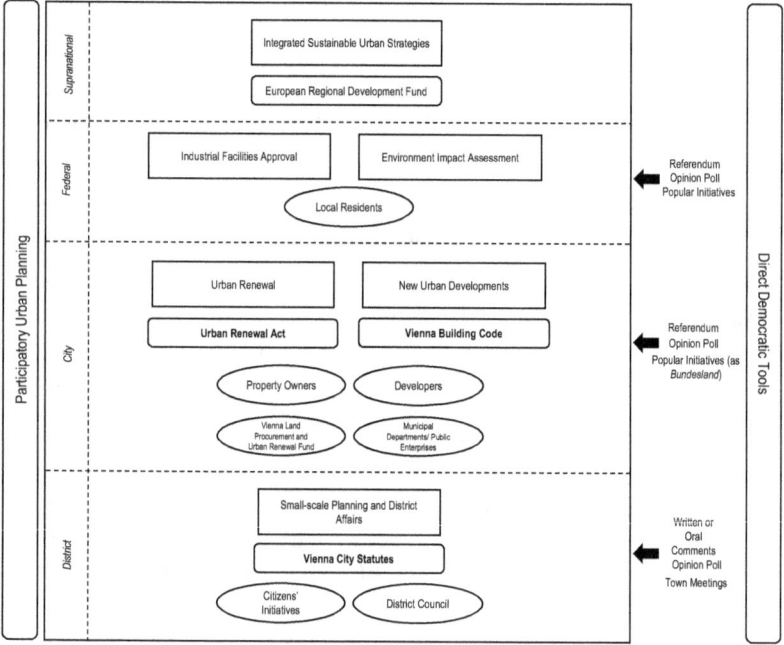

Figure 3.1 Institutional pathways to formal participation in urban development in Vienna.

Source: European Commission (2014); Hammer (2014); Municipal Department 21 (2017), Author's own elaboration.

administration, which divided the existing planning department into districts, and shifted from partial to full decision-making power in land procurement and planning management to public enterprises, such as the Vienna Land Procurement and Urban Renewal Fund (see Figure 3.1).

Process innovation involving non-institutional actors coincided with growing global awareness of sustainable urban development, especially after the Rio Declaration and Agenda 21 in 1992, which urged local governments to expand public participation in the local decision-making process. Despite strategic plans for implementing a Local Agenda 21 in the late 1990s, the institutional effort to create a city-wide framework for localised grassroots participation never materialised under the Social-Democratic/Conservative coalition government. Unlike other European cities, for example in Sweden (Feichtinger and Pregernig, 2005) and the United Kingdom (Mittler, 2001), where the adoption of local agendas were organised in a top-down manner by local authorities, new opportunities for bottom-up mobilisation emerged in Vienna in 1998 through a further shift towards localised decision-making at the district level. Despite being rejected at the City level, the concrete interest in inclusion through bottom-up initiatives at the district level, in addition to assigning greater budget responsibility at the district level, initiated a pilot agenda process in the district of *Alsergrund* in 1998. The collaboration between this bottom-up initiative, *Local Agenda 21 Alsergrund*, and the district authorities, not only facilitated the active participation of local residents in neighbourhood planning, but also set new methodological standards for localised urban projects at the district level based on horizontal organisation of the planning process. Growing institutional recognition of the importance of community participation enabled citizens' initiatives to formulate planning concepts, as well as means to control and manage the process, together with the relevant municipal departments and private stakeholders. Such measures ultimately enabled citizens to influence the decision-making in the neighbourhood planning process (Novy and Hammer, 2007). This collaborative arrangement between citizens' initiatives, local residents and authorities became the City's organisational model for the Local Agenda 21 in 2002.

Another step towards localised collaborative arrangements emerged with the reorientation of the City's urban renewal strategies in the light of further decentralisation of public management under the same coalition government. Following the New Public Management precepts for output-oriented public services, the Urban Renewal Offices adopted a more active position in conflict management between different key stakeholders in urban redevelopment. Accordingly, two pilot renewal projects were carried out in the districts of *Brigittenau* and *Leopoldstadt* between 2000 and 2006, partially subsidised by the European Social Fund and the Regional Development Fund. In contrast to the City's local agenda process, the new collaboration between institutional and non-institutional actors in these renewal works was vertically managed, whereby co-management between different municipal bodies and public enterprises was prioritised over bottom-up residential participation. This mechanism was partly set up to meet the EU's funding criteria based on economic performance, rather than grassroots involvement. As such, the participation of community-based initiatives in the planning process was limited. As a result, the role of local residents and the Urban Renewal Office remained consultative, whereas the decision-making authority in two urban renewal zones was expanded to the City's Economic Development Fund and the Municipal Department for European Affairs (Novy et al., 2010). As the renewal objectives largely focused on the economic development of neighbourhoods in decline, process innovation in these pilot projects drew on the flexibilisation of the City's renewal management structure, whereby the collaboration between key stakeholders at different territorial levels could occur beyond their institutional boundaries.

Despite limited innovation in bottom-up participation in urban renewal, the Urban Renewal Offices still remain the main coordinator of public dialogue between relevant institutional actors and residents in neighbourhood redevelopment, whereas the Local Agenda 21 Offices offer a bottom-up pathway for active participation in localised small-scale urban projects. Therefore, a mix of bottom-up and top-down participatory pathways in urban planning continue to characterise the collaborative arrangement between institutional and non-institutional actors in the overall institutional landscape of Vienna. However, the degree of recognition of local stakeholders and representation of their interests in the planning process is largely limited to the particular territorial level at which direct citizen participation in broader urban issues is continually constrained by its institutional design and the existing socioeconomic structure.

The collaborative arrangement for active citizenship and its context

Currently, coordination of bottom-up participatory processes at the neighbourhood level continues through the Local Agenda 21 and the Urban Renewal Offices. The former coordinates bottom-up pathways of active participation in neighbourhood planning, whereby citizens' initiatives formulate and manage planning concepts and methods that concern the sustainable development of their own district. More recently, a few efforts to overcome bureaucratic hurdles led to the implementation of new pathways for citizens' initiatives to directly participate in neighbourhood planning. In 2015, a new participatory program (*Grätzeloase*), initiated by the Local Agenda 21 Office and the city administration, was launched to activate citizen participation in co-production of non-market public spaces and communal activities at the district level. This involved two rounds of revision by the municipal departments, the district authorities, the police and the Chamber of Commerce. The emphasis on self-organisation in urban development at the local level is also visible in the growing number of *Do-It-Yourself* activities, such as urban gardening, food networks and repair activities, set forward by the Urban Renewal Offices (Jonas and Segert, 2019). Whilst continuing its primary function as the local coordination office for on-site conflict management in target planning areas, the Urban Renewal Offices have adopted a non-market-based 'commoning' approach to citizen participation, where extensive sharing and learning processes can be fostered within the public-citizens partnership in a non-hierarchical fashion. Accordingly, the trend towards self-organisation, based on a combination of bottom-up mobilisation and a top-down institutional framework, expanded across the city. Since January 2020, the Local Agenda process takes place in 11 out of 23 districts in Vienna.

The availability of bottom-up pathways to direct participation at the district level is determined by the respective district council, which is not only responsible for small-scale neighbourhood planning, but also decides whether to implement and finance (50%) the Local Agenda process. Given this local anchor, incorporation of bottom-up initiatives in neighbourhood planning largely depends on the local political dynamics. The competition-based project selection method, especially in *Grätzeloase*, therefore, aimed at reshaping the political boundaries of self-organisation in urban development. Unlike the regular selection criteria of the Local Agenda 21 Office, any individual can submit community-oriented projects with a focus on public space revitalisation, which are then evaluated by a jury of relevant municipal departments. This 'commoning' approach to neighbourhood planning has expanded the alternative pathways for non-institutional actors to engage at the district level from 33 in 2015 to 83 in 2019.

The extent of local co-production in *Grätzeloase*, however, has been largely limited by its organisational model, which falls short of addressing the existing inequalities among neighbourhoods (Brait and Hammer, 2017). In addition to the competition-based selection method that diminishes the deliberative potential of the 'commoning' approach, a lack of appropriate public interventions to address the existing inequalities has led to the spatial concentration of self-organisation in neighbourhood planning (see Figure 3.2). In other words, participatory practices tend to be clustered in urban areas, where average earnings and educational attainment are relatively high compared to other districts, and participatory opportunities are already available. For example, an uneven spatial distribution of bottom-up urban initiatives is particularly visible in the district of *Neubau* (7th), with the second highest share of the population with tertiary education (47.2% in 2017), and where most *Grätzeloase* projects have been initiated by the local businesses on large commercial streets. Whilst the local engagement of cultural and social associations is more frequent in the districts of *Rudolfsheim-Fünfhaus* (15th) and *Hernals* (17th), the local agenda groups take an active role in securing *Grätzeloase* projects in the districts of *Josefstadt* (8th), *Favoriten* (10th), and *Währing* (18th), where bottom-up channels for participation are already available to citizens' initiatives by the districts' Agenda offices. A lack of both top-down and bottom-up pathways to participation is particularly visible in the district of *Simmering* (11th), governed by the FPÖ between 2015 and 2020, where (as of 2017) the share of the population with tertiary education (12.7%) and the median income (20,568 EUR) are one of the lowest in the city (Statistics Vienna, 2020). The lack of an appropriate framework that could guide bottom-up practices in addressing the existing local inequalities has also engendered a low degree of thematic diversity. Whilst expanding opportunities for grassroots mobilisation enable citizens' initiatives to actively formulate and realise small-scale urban projects at the neighbourhood level, this contracting-out practice undermines horizontal networks of decision-making, in which the interests of different stakeholders are recognised and represented. As the city government retreats to a steering role in bottom-up participation of community-based initiatives, missing interactive mechanisms in direct participatory platforms has exacerbated event-based public-citizen collaboration, dominated by low-cost 'pop-up' urban projects, led by a limited number of civil society actors, which pay little attention to the place-specific contexts.

Whilst the capacity for bottom-up practices of co-production in neighbourhood planning lies at the district level, the localised planning system at the City level supplements the lack of participation opportunities in the districts, where the Local Agenda 21 is absent. Some

Unlocking the door of the city hall 45

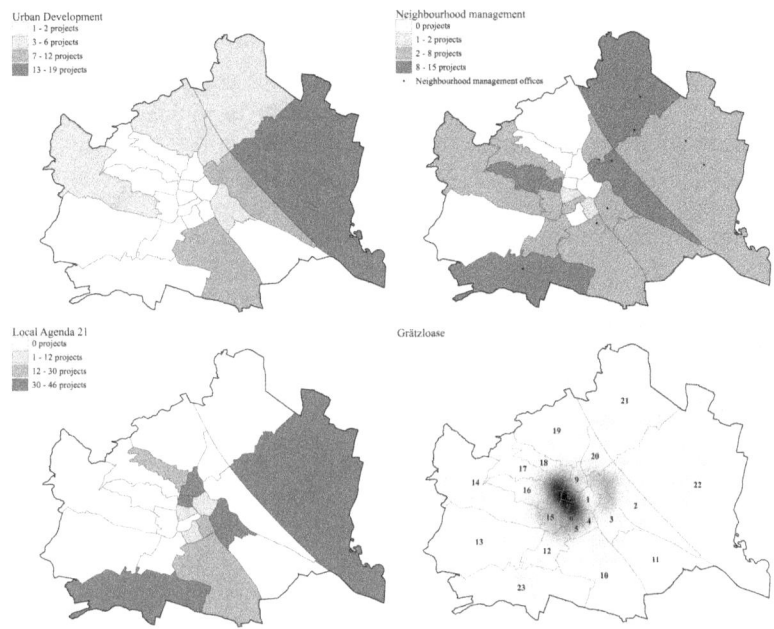

Figure 3.2 Geographical distribution of participatory channels in urban development in Vienna, 2020.
Source: Urban Renewal Office; Local Agenda 21, Author's own elaboration.

districts have particularly benefited from this institutional complementarity: namely, the underprivileged outer-city districts, such as *Leopoldstadt* (2nd), *Ottakring* (16th) and *Floridsdorf* (21st), where existing participatory channels are mostly organised by the local Urban Renewal Offices. Since 2012, the Urban Renewal Office expanded its role in new development areas, where the newly established Neighbourhood Management Offices coordinate participatory processes to accommodate the respective interests of old and new residents. Despite growing – and diversified – indirect participatory channels in localised urban projects, the extent of public-citizens partnership in new development areas is limited by the Vienna Building Code, which only grants direct control over the formal planning processes to property owners (see Figure 3.1). This is a distinct weakness in the City's participatory framework: its strong top-down orientation and its nearly exclusive role in urban planning results in limited citizen empowerment within the formal decision-making processes. Such a top-down and interventionist policy approach is an enduring legacy of the long Social-Democratic municipal government, which has provided limited support to civic involvement in public affairs. Whilst the Urban Renewal Offices and the Neighbourhood Management Offices provide local residents with opportunities for inclusion, engagement and deliberation in the planning processes, these participatory channels lack a policy framework to ensure that participation has a meaningful impact in policy implementation. Currently, there is no adequate policy framework to empower localised bottom-up practices in a diverse range of policy fields, other than urban planning, where local residents can make a substantial contribution to the outcome of the decision-making process beyond tokenistic participation.

Conclusions

In this chapter, we have shed light on the evolution of Vienna's urban development policy, and how the role of citizens in the localised planning system has changed throughout the period considered. From the early 1970s onwards, the City of Vienna has experimented with a diverse range of participatory tools, emerging from the decentralisation process, to encourage bottom-up mobilisation of community-based initiatives and the inclusion of non-institutional actors at different territorial levels of urban development. Whilst urban policies promoting citizen participation exist across cities and regions, the Vienna Model was particularly successful at linking non-institutional actors to the formal policy-making structure and limiting the potential interference of market actors. The longstanding decentralisation process downscaled substantial power and resources to public enterprises and district authorities, opening up top-down participatory pathways from 'informing' and 'consultation' to – limited degrees of – citizen power. Simultaneously, this rescaling process allowed both the city administration and its districts to enhance grassroots engagement at the neighbourhood level, allowing local residents to actively participate in designing and evaluating community planning projects. Whilst the opportunities grew, however, such standardisation and formalisation have compounded the bureaucratic obstacles to activate the participation of broader social groups. Some attempts have been made to circumvent this bureaucratic tendency. However, our analysis points out that the increased participation of organised community actors went hand in hand with negative side-effects of self-organisation in small-scale neighbourhood planning, resulting in the uneven distribution of participatory channels.

The latter are mainly concentrated around the city's inner-city districts, where educational attainment and median earnings are relatively high. Our findings, therefore, echo some concerns raised by participation scholars: the literature in the field has warned about the potential self-selection of individuals with higher cultural, social and economic resources taking part in participatory initiatives (Fung, 2015). The uneven distribution of bottom-up initiatives across the city casts light on exclusionary processes engendered by participation policies in Vienna. This issue is mainly due to two factors, which may appear to be at odds with one another at face value. First, an over-regulation and bureaucratisation of participatory policy, which stifles citizens' engagement in planning. Second, the lack of a proper policy framework – if not political willingness – enshrining fully fledge participation. This policy deficit hinders meaningful involvement of citizens, falling short of empowering them. Therefore, the regulatory excess, coupled with the absence of a truly empowering participatory policy approach, seems to confirm the description of the Viennese municipal governance in the literature as a bureaucratic and top-down system. In turn, such a top-down approach fails to design interventions that reflect each neighbourhood's specific context. Ultimately, our analysis hints at increasing citizen participation in the planning process at different scales. The expansion of public participation, however, has been less successful in reducing unequal access to adequate representation for all and curbing the still strong intervention of the city administration. It appears that Vienna acts as a controlling enabler, reluctantly letting go of their exclusive oversight in the planning process. So far, we are yet to witness mechanisms that overcome participatory injustices emanating from Vienna's existing intraurban inequalities

Note

1 The construction of the conference complex around the United Nations was highly controversial in the 1980s, pushed by the SPÖ in the federal government, despite a failed legislative referral in 1981 and a popular initiative in 1982.

References

Antalovsky, E. and König, I., 1994. *Planung initiativ: Bürgerbeteiligung in Wien.* [pdf] Available at: https://bit.ly/3mLduQ2 [Accessed 14 April 2021].

Arnstein, S.R., 1969. A ladder of citizen participation. *Journal of the American Institute of Planners,* 35(4), pp. 216–224.

Berger, H., 1984. *Gebietserneuerung 1974–1984: Das Wiener Modell.* [pdf] Available at: https://bit.ly/32aVh5f [Accessed 14 April 2021].

Brait, R. and Hammer, K., 2017. The Viennese Grätzloase: The role of the commons in countering market-based transformations of the city. *Der Öffentliche Sektor – The Public Sector,* 43(1), pp. 33–43.

Dangeschat, J.S. and Hamedinger, A., 2009. Planning culture in Austria: The case of Vienna, the unlike city. In: Knieling, J. and Othengrafen, F., eds., 2009. *Planning cultures in Europe: Decoding cultural phenomena in urban and regional planning.* Florence: Taylor and Francis, pp. 95–112.

Davies, J.S., 2004. Conjuncture or disjuncture? An institutionalist analysis of local regeneration partnerships in the UK. *International Journal of Urban and Regional Research,* 28(3), pp. 570–585.

Elwood, S., 2004. Partnerships and participation: Reconfiguring urban governance in different state contexts. *Urban Geography,* 25(8), pp. 755–770.

European Commission, 2014. Integrated Sustainable Urban Development. Cohesion Policy 2014-2020. [pdf] Available at: https://ec.europa.eu/regional_policy/sources/docgener/informat/2014/urban_en.pdf

Feichtinger, J. and Pregernig, M., 2005. Imagined citizens and participation: Local Agenda 21 in two communities in Sweden and Austria. *Local Environment,* 10(3), pp. 229–242.

Feuerstein, C. and Fitz, A., 2009. *Wann begann temporär? Frühe Stadtinterventionen und sanfte Stadterneuerung in Wien.* Vienna: Springer-Verlag.

Förster, W., 1988. Stadterneuerung in Wien. In: Dase, M., Lüdtke, J. and Wollmann, H., eds., 1989. *Stadterneuerung im Wandel: Erfahrungen aus Ost und West.* Basel: Birkhäuser, pp. 103–114.

Fraser, N., 2010. *Scales of justice: Reimagining political space in a globalizing world.* New York: Columbia University Press.

Freisitzer, K. and Maurer, J., eds., 1985. *Das Wiener Modell: Erfahrungen mit innovativer Stadtplanung. Empirische Befunde aus einem Großprojekt.* Vienna: Compress.

Fung, A., 2015. Putting the public back into governance: The challenges of citizen participation and its future. *Public Administration Review,* 75(4), pp. 513–522.

Garcia, M., 2006. Citizenship practices and urban governance in European cities. *Urban Studies,* 43(4), pp. 745–765.

Goldfrank, B., 2007. The politics of deepening local democracy: Decentralization, party institutionalization, and participation. *Comparative Politics,* 39(2), pp. 147–168.

Hammer, K., 2014. BürgerInnenbeteiligung in der Stadt: Zwischen Demokratie und Ausgrenzung? *Stadtpunkte,* 9, Vienna. [pdf]Available at: https://wien.arbeiterkammer.at/service/studien/stadtpunkte/Stadtpunkte_9_.pdf

Jonas, M. and Segert, A. 2019. *Repair Und Do-It-Yourself Urbanism in Wien aus Bezirksperspektive.* [pdf] Available at: https://bit.ly/32aVfKw [Accessed 14 April 2021].

Kornberger, M., Meyer, R.E., Brandtner, C., et al., 2017. When bureaucracy meets the crowd: Studying "Open Government" in the Vienna City Administration. *Organization Studies,* 38(2), pp. 179–200.

Mayerhofer, P. and Wolfmayr-Schnitzer, Y., 1996. Wiens "neue" Rolle im europäischen Städtenetz: Chancen als spezialisiertes Dienstleistungszentrum in Mitteleuropa? *Wirtschaft und Gesellschaft*, 22(4), pp. 515–551.

Mattl, S., 2000. *Das 20. Jahrhundert. Geschichte Wiens*. Vienna: Pichler Verlag.

Mittler, D., 2001. Hijacking sustainability? Planners and the promise and failure of local agenda 21. In: Layard, A., Davoudi, S. and Batty, S., eds., 2001. *Planning for a sustainable future*. London: Taylor & Francis, pp. 53–60.

Municipal Department 21 - District Planning and Land Use, 2017. Masterplan Partizipative Stadtentwicklung: Frühzeitiges Beteiligen der Bevölkerung an städtebaulichen Planungs- und Widmungsprozessen. *Werkstattbericht der Stadtentwicklung Wien*, 172, Vienna. [pdf] Available at: https://www.wien.gv.at/stadtentwicklung/studien/pdf/b008505.pdf

Novy, A. and Hammer, E., 2007. Radical innovation in the era of liberal governance. *European Urban and Regional Studies*, 14(3), pp. 210–222.

Novy, A., Hammer, E. and Leubolt, B., 2010. The limits of 'controlled modernisation': The Grätzelmanagement experience in Vienna. In: Moulaert, F., Swyngedouw, E., Martinelli, F. and Gonzalez, S., eds., 2010. *Can neighbourhoods save the city? Community development and social innovation*. London: Routledge, pp. 185–197.

Novy, A., Redak, V., Jäger, J., et al., 2001. The end of Red Vienna. *European Urban and Regional Studies*, 8(2), pp. 131–144.

Pleschberger, W. and Mertens, C., 2012. Zur Parteipolitisierung Der Direkten Kommunalen Demokratie: Am Beispiel Der Großstadt Wien. *Mitteilungen des Instituts für Deutsches und Internationales Parteienrecht und Parteienforschung*, 18, pp. 24–35.

Schimak, G., 1993. Weltausstellung 1995 Wien. Budapest. Ursachen Und Konsequenzen Der Absage Wiens. In: Häußermann H., and Siebel W., eds., 1993. *Festivalisierung Der Stadtpolitik. Stadtentwicklung Durch Große Projekte*. Wiesbaden: Verlag für Sozialwissenschaften, pp. 108–133.

Statistics Vienna, 2020. *Vienna in Figures*. [pdf] Available at: https://bit.ly/3v2HASn [Accessed 14 April 2021].

Suitner, J., 2020. Vienna's planning history: Periodizing stable phases of regulating urban development, 1820–2020. *Planning Perspectives*, pp. 1–22. https://doi.org/10.1080/02665433.2020.1862700

Teaford, J.C., 2000. Urban renewal and its aftermath. *Housing Policy Debate*, 11(2), pp. 443–465.

Zhang, L., Lin, Y., Hooimeijer, P., et al., 2020. Heterogeneity of public participation in urban redevelopment in Chinese cities: Beijing versus Guangzhou. *Urban Studies,* 57(9), pp. 1903–1919.

Part II
Housing

4 Affordable housing for all? Challenging the legacy of Red Vienna

Katharina Litschauer and Michael Friesenecker

Introduction

Housing plays a particularly important role in social inclusion and urban justice, as it influences urban segregation and profoundly shapes people's living conditions. Similar to other European cities, such as Amsterdam, it has been argued that Vienna's particularly large, de-commodified housing stock contributes to affordable housing for a wide section of the population. This model of *housing for all* builds upon the achievements of *Red Vienna* and is characterised by both a large social rental segment as well as strict rent control in the private rental segment. Since social housing competes directly with private rental housing, affordable housing is also achieved by dampening rent levels in the private segment. Hence, both social and private rental provide affordable housing.

However, like other European cities, Vienna is increasingly facing affordability problems that challenge its *housing for all* approach. Demographic change, immigration, rising income inequality, property price increases and housing policy deregulations put pressure on housing affordability and urban justice. Such pressures are similarly experienced by many cities, though these pressures can be mediated in quite distinct ways depending on the historical trajectory and concrete policy choices of the respective city. Over the past decade, population growth and migration increased demand for housing in Vienna and changed the urban context of housing policy. In addition, two policy shifts affected the provision of affordable housing: the delegation of social housing construction to limited-profit housing associations, and the deregulation of rent controls in the private rental segment (Kadi, 2015). Against this background, this chapter explores how policy shifts and changing urban conditions are affecting housing affordability in Vienna and elaborates on underlying mechanisms that threaten the city's *housing for all* approach.

DOI: 10.4324/9781003133827-6

Regarding European cities, research in urban studies has analysed how housing policy reforms – such as homeownership promotion, privatisation of social housing and de-regulation of rent control – have contributed to tenure restructurings and transformed housing systems (van Duijne and Ronald, 2018; Stephens, 2020). Applying the concept of *regulated marketisation*, Hochstenbach and Ronald (2020) reveal how and why a revival of private rental took place in Amsterdam. In a similar vein, van Duijne and Ronald's (2018) study of Amsterdam shows how the unitary rental market has been unravelling by exploring processes of *dualisation* between social and private housing. Research on Vienna's housing system has highlighted the integrated nature of its rental market (Mundt and Amann, 2010), analysed the state of social housing and current challenges in Vienna (Mundt, 2018), and investigated changes in social housing policy (Lévy-Vroelant and Reinprecht, 2014). Another strand of research assesses how policy reforms impact on housing conditions rather than the housing system (Kadi and Musterd, 2014; Kadi, 2015). Kadi and Musterd (2014) study the effects of reforms on accessibility and affordability in Amsterdam, whilst Kadi (2015) explores housing conditions for low-income households in Vienna and asked how policy reforms produced insiders and outsiders regarding access to affordable housing.

Building on these findings, we analyse shifts in Vienna's housing system in terms of the city's status as a *just city* by going beyond low-income households and asking who (still) has access to affordable and secure housing. Drawing on Fainstein's (2010) analytical framework of *equity* and *recognition*, we analyse how access to affordable housing has shifted over time. *Recognition* focuses on the design of policies, drawing attention to the acknowledgement of tenant rights in (private) rental housing as well as changing eligibility criteria and existing access barriers in social rental housing. *Equity* refers to '[the] distribution of both material and nonmaterial benefits derived from public policy' (Fainstein, 2010, p. 36). In the context of housing, this calls for an analysis of housing costs and security in different sub-segments of the Viennese housing system.

To analyse the distributional outcomes, we draw on the concept of *dualisation*, understood as an increasing differentiation of 'rights, entitlements, and services' (Emmenegger, 2012, p. 10) to grasp the split between access to, and exclusion from, affordable and secure housing. Contrary to existing research that either focuses on a 'split forged between social and private housing under dualization' (van Duijne and Ronald, 2018, p. 637) or 'a dualization trend among low-income households' (Kadi, 2015, p. 247), we apply it to housing conditions (more specifically housing costs and tenure security). This allows us to give a more nuanced picture of the implications of tenure, identify increasingly less affordable and secure sub-segments within both private and social rental, and specify in which regard an unbalancing of segments is taking place. The result of this dualisation is both a gap between affordable and unaffordable housing (structural outcome) and a gap between insiders and outsiders (social outcome). Analysing tenant profiles in sub-segments shows who has access to affordable sub-segments and which groups are locked out.

Accordingly, the next section outlines how recognition has changed by presenting the historical trajectory of Vienna's housing policy as well as recent policy reforms. Subsequently, we attend to the outcomes of housing policy and analyse processes of dualisation by investigating tenure restructuring, housing cost developments and changes in tenure security. In addition, we draw attention to insider-outsider divides by analysing shifts in tenant profiles and highlighting who has access to affordable sub-segments. This allows us to assess the city's redistributive capacities and evaluate how just the housing system of Vienna still is.

Shifts in housing policy: the legacy of *Red Vienna* and its transformation

Today's housing policy in Austria came into existence after the Second World War and was developed within a framework of social policy and not only as a response to housing (market) problems (Matznetter, 2002). Housing policy contributes to high-quality and affordable housing by relying on three key pillars: first, acknowledging housing as a basic right. Housing regulations traditionally exert rent controls, especially in the private rental market. Second, social housing continues to be highly important, is targeted at a broad section of the population, and provided by both municipalities and *limited-profit housing associations* (LPHAs). LPHAs are well-established actors in the Austrian housing system and are required to charge cost-covering rents in exchange for tax exemptions (for details see Chapter 5 by Friesenecker and Litschauer in this volume). Third, housing subsidies – especially for new constructions – are an important element in steering housing construction and securing affordable housing, whilst housing allowances play a less important role.

Housing policy in Austria is highly complex and embedded in a historically grown, multilevel setting. The general responsibility for housing lies at the federal level and includes the Tenancy Law and legislation regarding LPHAs. Vienna, being both a *Bundesland* and a municipality, not only provides social housing (i.e. municipal housing) but also has full autonomy regarding housing subsidies. Hence, whilst rent controls (first pillar) are a federal competence, both the federal and the local level influence social housing (second pillar), and housing subsidies are the sole responsibility of the City.

However, over the past decades, two housing policy reforms have profoundly influenced Vienna's capacity to provide affordable housing. First, at the local level, Vienna shifted social housing construction from municipal to limited-profit housing associations; and second, at the national level, private rental housing was deregulated.

Social housing: from municipal to limited-profit housing

Vienna has a long history of promoting socially inclusive forms of urban development (see Chapter 3 by Ahn and Mocca in this volume). During the *Red Vienna* era of the 1920s, the local state established itself as a forerunner in social housing, and although the policy focus has shifted over the decades, the social democratic principles of housing policy still remain (for more discussion on Social Democracy, see Chapter 2 by Mocca and Friesenecker in this volume). The 'Viennese Model' of taking 'responsibility for the provision of efficient infrastructure, municipal services and, in particular, for affordable housing' continues to this day (see STEP 2025, 2014). Contrary to most European cities, Vienna still administers a large municipal housing sector. In addition, social housing is also provided by LPHAs. Together, the two sub-segments of social housing deliver affordable and secure housing for a broad section of the population (almost half of all residencies in Vienna, see below).

Although Vienna never sold its municipal housing stock, new constructions were phased out in the mid-1990s and ceased in 2004. Whilst municipal housing construction was reintroduced in 2016, only 4,000 units are currently under construction, therefore handing the task of social housing construction to LPHAs. The retreat was justified in reference to limits on public debt due to European regulations (Maastricht criteria and Competition Law), and it was argued that LPHAs offer comparable low rents. Although it seems like a viable alternative, it differs from municipal housing in some important respects.

First, rent setting differs. In municipal housing, legally set rent applies, whereas rent in limited-profit housing is cost-covering and depends on the respective land, building and financing costs. As shown below, in practice, rents are comparable and both sub-segments guarantee affordable housing. A crucial difference, however, are the down payments required by tenants in limited-profit housing. Depending on land and financing costs, the average down payment is 500 €/m^2 (approx. 40,000 EUR for an 80 m^2 flat), which is returned to tenants when they move out (discounted yearly by 1%). This poses an important access barrier to limited-profit housing, especially for low-income households, and implies a shift in recognition, with distributional consequences for households with little financial resources.

Second, eligibility criteria differ. High income thresholds give broad sections of the population (nearly 80%) formal access to limited-profit housing, guaranteeing a social mix and preventing segregation (net annual income for a single household is 47,000 EUR, and for a family with two children it is 90,000 EUR). Municipal housing is more targeted, as additional criteria apply. Whilst only Austrian citizens were eligible for municipal housing up until 2006, non-EU residents gained access after five years of legal residency (i.e. *equivalent citizens*) following the EU directive on the equal treatment of third-country nationals. The change in the policy design has therefore led to the recognition of the housing needs of non-Austrian citizens and strengthened Vienna's *housing for all* approach. In 2015, the allocation policy for municipal housing was reformed once again. Henceforth, Austrian or equivalent citizens over the age of 17 who are within the income limits and have lived at their current Viennese address for at least two years are eligible for subsidised (limited-profit) housing, allocated by the City. For municipal housing and SMART apartments (see below), a justified housing need must also be demonstrated. Hence, the target group of municipal housing are young adults (up to the age of 30), single parents, and people in social hardship (overcrowding, illness etc.). In light of increasing demand for social housing, the City's approach to new lettings became more targeted, making access for (long-term) migrants with non-Austrian Citizenship easier.

Third, since LPHAs are regulated at the national level, this weakens Vienna's steering capacity. By retreating from municipal housing construction, the City has progressively lost its capacity to influence new construction and allocate social housing in accordance with its own target groups. However, the granting of housing subsidies gives the City the right to allocate one-third of newly constructed units for the duration of the subsidy loan (40 years). Additionally, housing subsidies allow the City to realise objectives by adjusting subsidy schemes. The so-called *SMART apartment* model was introduced in 2012 to better serve low-income households. Down payments for these are limited (approx. 5,000 EUR for an 80 m^2 flat) and compact floor plans reduce housing costs (for further details, see Chapter 5 by Friesenecker and Litschauer in this volume). The City of Vienna stipulates that half of all subsidised dwellings must be SMART apartments. Thus, Vienna did not completely lose its redistributive capacities, but rather shifted them from active provision to steering via housing subsidies. This model has allowed the City to reduce differences in rent setting and eligibility/access between the two sub-segments of social housing. Whilst policy instruments have changed, the overall approach of *housing for all* remains and continues to target broad sections of the population, whilst also providing for those in need. Vienna continues its commitment to providing affordable municipal housing and steers new construction in limited-profit housing via housing subsidies. However, redistributive capacities differ between the two sub-segments of social housing, especially regarding eligibility, access and housing costs. This creates the potential for housing conditions to drift apart.

Private rental: deregulation of rent controls

Affordable housing is not only provided by social rental housing, but also rests on strict rent controls in the private rental segment. Implemented as part of the post-war Keynesian welfare strategy, rent controls apply to housing units built before 1945, accounting for around two-thirds of private rental and 42% of total rental (Kadi, 2015). However, the last three decades saw profound deregulation and a dismantling of tenant rights in private rental housing. The harmonisation and simplification of housing regulation was a consensual goal in the political discourse of the early 1990s and was followed by further liberalisations by the conservative/right-wing national government (ÖVP-FPÖ) at the beginning of the 21st century.

Within the rent-controlled segment, the amendment of the Tenancy Law of 1993 (legally effective in 1994) was the most substantial reform. Whilst the rent in rent-controlled dwellings was set according to pre-defined categories regarding the standard of amenities (so-called *category rent*), the amendment introduced the so-called *reference value rent* for rental contracts signed after 1994. In addition to the standard of amenities, the amendment allowed private landlords to charge location premiums. Location premiums are not legally set, but recommendations provided by the City and legally binding only in case of controversy. Location premiums are adjusted according to building plot prices in the respective area and have increased sharply over the last decade. Whilst location premiums remained stable until 2010 (approx. 1 €/m^2 in good locations), they now range between 1.50 and 4.60 €/m^2, depending on the location. However, following a Supreme Court decision in 2018, Vienna introduced a new calculation logic that classifies only one-third of all rent-controlled dwellings as above average, effectively reducing rent levels by evading location premiums. Hence, whilst the policy design at the national level strengthened the profit interests of owners, the City continues to recognise tenant rights and tries to secure housing affordability also in the private rental segment.

Furthermore, the amendment of 1993 introduced time-limited rental agreements. Initially this aimed at short-term increases in housing supply, as the maximum duration could not exceed ten years and a 20% discount on the rent applied. However, with the amendment of the Tenancy Law in 2000, the maximum duration was abolished, and henceforth a 25% discount applied. In addition, the conservative/right-wing national government (ÖVP-FPÖ) excluded detached and semi-detached dwellings, as well as attic conversions from the Tenancy Law regulation at the turn of the millennium. This implies that rent controls and regulation of contracts no longer apply, thereby reducing the rent-controlled segment. Hence, within private rental, housing is progressively framed as a commodity rather than a basic need, tenant rights are abolished and rent controls evaded.

The reforms of the Tenancy Law saw the layering of new policies onto existing ones, as new regulations only apply for new contracts. Reforms shifted recognition in private rental and created the potential for housing conditions to drift apart. Housing costs in rent-controlled private housing now depend on the date of the rental agreement and land price developments, whilst the introduction of time-limited contracts potentially leads to tenure insecurity. Therefore, although the overall approach remains, shifts in recognition indicate diminishing redistributive capacities. Whether policy reforms led to changing distributional outcomes will be analysed in the next section.

Trends of dualisation in affordable and secure housing

Following the assessment of housing policy shifts in both social and private rental, we can now evaluate whether this led to processes of dualisation of housing conditions in the Viennese housing system. More specifically, we analyse processes of tenure restructuring and tenure security, and evaluate housing cost developments.

Tenure restructuring and tenure security

Whilst clear shifts in tenure were reported in relation to other European cities (Andersson and Turner, 2014; van Duijne and Ronald, 2018), Vienna's tenure structure remained rather stable between 1991 and 2018. Overall, the number of dwellings increased, but the rental sector consistently accounts for over 70% of main residencies, compared to homeownership standing at less than 20% (see Table 4.1). In contrast, in Amsterdam, owner-occupied housing increased from 12% in 1998 to 32% in 2017 and declined to 31% in 2019 (Hochstenbach and Ronald, 2020). In Vienna, the rental segment splits nearly equally into private and social housing, whilst social housing even increased slightly between 1991 and 2018 to 43% of all dwellings, and 57% of rental housing. This suggests that social housing is still highly important and competes with private rental housing. However, within social housing, a shift from municipal to limited-profit housing is observable. Whilst the City still owns over 20% of the total housing stock, LPHAs increased their share of rental housing from 16% to almost 28%. Considering access barriers in limited-profit housing, this indicates a differentiation of rights between sub-segments of social housing and thus a process of dualisation.

Table 4.1 Tenure structure Vienna, 1991–2018

	1991°		2018		% change 1991°– 2018
	(%) of main residence	(%) of rental	(%) of main residence	(%) of rental	
Main segments					
Ownership	17.4		19.4		2.0
Rental	73.6		76.3		2.8
Other*	9.0		4.2		-4.8
Rental subsegments					
Social rental	39.4	53.6	43.4	56.8	3.9
Municipal housing	27.5	37.4	22.2	29.0	-5.4
Limited-profit housing	11.9	16.2	21.2	27.8	9.3
Private rental	34.2	46.4	33.0	43.2	-1.2
Rent-controlled[+]	31.2	42.4	22.2	29.1	-9.0
Free market rent	3.0	4.1	10.8	14.1	7.8
Time-limited°	4.0	5.4	13.2	17.3	9.2
Unlimited°	33.9	45.0	19.8	26.0	-14.2

Sources: 1991 – STATISTIK AUSTRIA, Dwelling and Building Register; 2005 and 2018 – Austrian Microcensus; weighted analysis, own calculation; N=11,850 (2005), N=11,050 (2018).
Note: *service accommodation, free of charge, etc.; [+]approximated as dwellings in buildings built before 1944; °for time-limited and unlimited contracts 2005–2018.

Besides social housing, rent-controlled private rental also offers affordable housing. Whereas the share of private rental remained rather stable, the share of rent-controlled housing decreased significantly. In 1991, almost all private rental dwellings were rent controlled (93%). By 2018, the share of the free market rent sub-segment had increased to 33% of private rental (14% of total rental). This change can be explained in reference to newly added private rental housing, the demolition of old stock and the exclusion of attic conversations from regulation.

Furthermore, the introduction of time-limited contracts in 1994 established sub-segments in private rental housing that are characterised by diverging housing conditions with regard to tenure security. Contrary to both sub-segments of social housing, which provide unlimited rental agreements, the 1994 amendment jeopardises tenure security in private rental. Only 5% of rental contracts were time-limited in 2005 (11% of private rental), however, this increased to 17% in 2018 (40% of private rental). In the free market sub-segment, the share even increased from 12% to 55% between 2005 and 2018. This suggests a dualisation of housing conditions in rental housing with regard to tenure security that is even more pronounced in the free market segment. Taking account of the fact that 67% of new contracts in private rental are time limited (Tockner, 2017), it becomes apparent that obtaining unlimited private rental is becoming increasingly difficult. The social outcome of this dualisation regarding tenure security within private rental is an evolving insider-outsider divide, with sitting tenants enjoying long-term, secure housing, whilst newcomers face increasingly insecure, time-limited contracts.

As social housing still offers unlimited contracts, the introduction of time-limited contracts in private rental also results in an increasing dualisation between private and social rental. Tockner (2017) reports that 60% of all new rental agreements are in the private market (only 22% in municipal, and 18% in limited-profit housing), which indicates that obtaining social rental housing is becoming increasingly difficult. The social outcome of this dualisation is that social housing tenants are insiders to tenure security, whilst others are progressively locked out.

Although no overall tenure restructuring took place in Vienna between 1991 and 2018, shifts *within* private rental indicate processes of dualisation regarding tenure security that forge a divide between newcomers and sitting tenants. This also brings the danger of a divide between social and private rental, although currently the majority of all rental contracts are still unlimited and social housing contributes to high levels of tenure security. The next section analyses trends of dualisation regarding housing costs in rental sub-segments.

Housing costs

In light of housing cost developments in the respective sub-segments, Figure 4.1 shows that levels and trends differ substantially. First, a divide in rental prices emerged between social and private rental. In 2005, prices were rather similar (5.1 and 5.4 €/m^2, respectively) but diverged by 2018 (7 and 9.8 €/m^2, respectively). By contrast, Kadi and Musterd (2014) report a median rent increase of only 28% for Amsterdam between 1995 and 2009.

Second, regarding the two sub-segments of social housing, it is apparent that rental prices in limited-profit housing were slightly higher than in municipal housing in 2005 and this continued until 2018. Considering down payments in limited-profit housing are not included in rental prices, municipal housing is, in practice, the most affordable segment. Nevertheless, since the trend is similar in both sub-segments, this suggests that no dualisation of rents within social housing took place.

Third, within private rental, a growing divide between the rent-controlled and the free market sub-segments is observable. Whilst free market rents soared from 5.9 €/m^2 in 2005 to 11.8 €/m^2 in 2018,

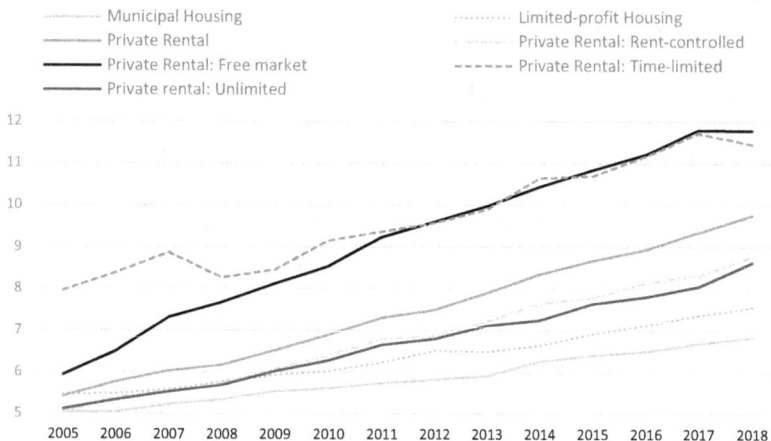

Figure 4.1 Development of rental prices in sub-segments.
Source: Statistik Austria; Microcensus 2005–2018, own calculations.
Note: *square meter rental prices, including utility costs. Rent controlled housing stock estimated as the private rental stock built before 1944

the increase in the rent-controlled sub-segment during the same period was less pronounced, from 5 to 8.8 €/m². Rent control effectively cushioned price developments, whilst liberalisations nevertheless increased costs. The introduction of location premiums in the rent-controlled segment transferred land price dynamics to the rent-controlled sub-segment, thereby increasing housing costs, especially since 2010. In addition, the introduction of time-limited rental agreements is another price driver. Although legally a 25% discount applies for time-limited contracts, paradoxically the rent level was already outstandingly high in 2005, at 7.9 €/m², and further increased to 11.5 €/m² in 2018. Since rental prices are renegotiated every three to five years, price dynamics on the overall housing market exert more pressure. Moreover, this indicates that rent controls are not enforced.

Policy reforms in private rental led to a dualisation of housing conditions, with tenure security and rent levels diverging in sub-segments. Whilst rent control still partly guarantees affordable housing, the free market sub-segment is becoming increasingly unaffordable. Boundaries between insiders and outsiders are redefined, forging a split between sitting tenants with old, unlimited contracts and newcomers to private rental housing that face insecure and more expensive housing conditions. In addition, access to social housing is becoming increasingly difficult, as down payments in limited-profit housing pose an access barrier and the percentage of new contracts in social housing is small. Meanwhile, sitting tenants in social housing enjoy secure and affordable housing conditions. The next section takes a closer look at tenant profiles in the respective housing sub-segments to elaborate on precisely who is affected by emerging divides in Viennese housing.

Who is affected by the affordable and secure housing divide?

Migration and rising income inequality are two main urban transformations that put pressure on housing affordability in Vienna. Figure 4.2 shows how income quintiles are distributed across sub-segments in 2011 and 2018 and additionally highlights changes in the distribution of citizenship (2005 and 2018).

Homeownership is dominated by high-income groups, and although private and social rental show a similar distribution of income groups, more low-income households are in private rental. Hence, private rental continues to be important for low-income groups, as they are overrepresented in this segment. Furthermore, they are slightly overrepresented in the free market sub-segment, and especially depend

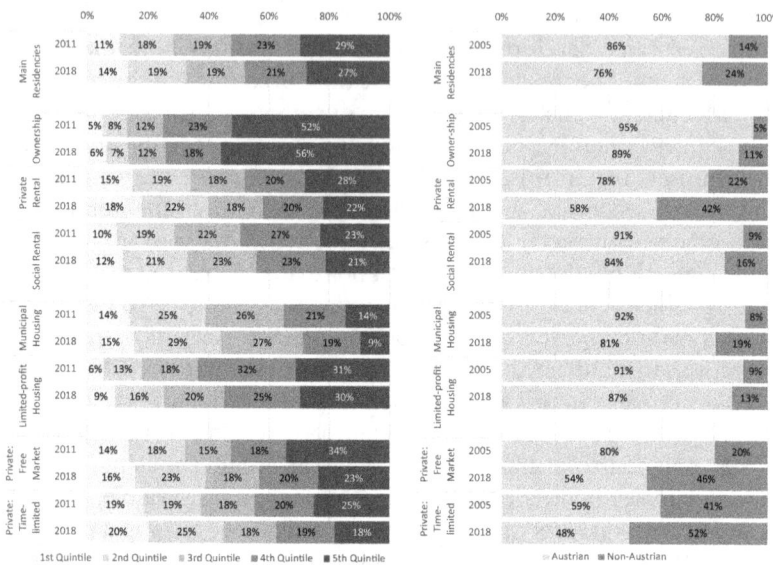

Figure 4.2 Tenant profiles – income quintiles (2011, 2018) and citizenship (2005, 2018) across tenures in Vienna.
Source: Statistik Austria; Microcensus 2005, 2011, 2018, own calculations. Net income per month and citizenship of household reference person.

on time-limited contracts. Considering recent housing cost developments, this indicates potential affordability problems for low-income groups. Data suggests that high-income households are leaving these more expensive sub-segments of private rental in favour of homeownership. Regarding social housing, no income group is profoundly over or underrepresented, confirming that social housing shows no signs of residualisation and continues to cater for a wide range of the population. However, a clear difference between municipal and limited-profit housing is observable, which suggests that down payments play out as access barriers. Whilst municipal housing is dominated by the second and third quintiles, limited-profit housing caters predominantly for mid- and high-income groups. Nevertheless, as the lowest two quintiles grew in limited-profit housing between 2011 and 2018, it seems that Vienna's housing subsidy policy (e.g. SMART apartments) leads to inclusion and redistribution.

As Vienna has faced major immigration since 1990, Figure 4.2 additionally highlights changes in the distribution of citizenship and shows that the share of non-Austrians increased from 14% to 24% between

2005 and 2018. Compared to their overall share, non-Austrians are underrepresented in homeownership (11% in 2018) and social rental (16% in 2018), whilst they are clearly and increasingly overrepresented in the private rental segment (42% in 2018). On closer inspection, they are increasingly dependent on the less affordable, free market sub-segment and time-limited contracts (46% and 52% in 2018), whereas the share of Austrians clearly dropped in free market rental. However, this does not necessarily imply affordability problems for all since, according to Kohlbacher and Reeger (2020), immigration is twofold. On the one hand, there are the well-educated immigrants and, on the other hand, the low- to mid-skilled immigrants who enter Vienna's labour and housing market (see Chapter 7 by Riederer, Verwiebe and Ahn in this volume). Nevertheless, as the share of non-Austrians in municipal housing increased, this indicates that the recognition of foreigners in 2006 led to inclusion and redistribution. Still, a higher share of non-Austrians are outsiders to affordable housing and face higher housing costs in the (free market) private rental segment. However, dualisation of housing conditions forges a split between insiders and outsiders that arises predominantly along residency (sitting tenants) rather than citizenship lines.

Conclusions

This chapter set out to evaluate Vienna's status as a *just city* by exploring access to affordable and secure housing. We analysed the development of housing conditions (housing costs and tenure security), presented how the split between affordable and unaffordable housing unfolds in Vienna, and showed who is affected by being locked out of affordable housing.

Though the City's *housing for all* model remains, shifts in recognition indicate changes in distributional outcomes. In private rental, the past decades saw profound liberalisations in Austria that have dismantled tenant rights and challenged the provision of affordable housing in Vienna. The introduction of location premiums and time-limited contracts in regulated private rental have diminished the redistributive capacity of rent controls. Housing conditions in private rental dualise both tenure security and housing costs, forging a split between affordable and unaffordable housing within the segment. In social rental, more vulnerable groups are targeted, and the opening to migrants has translated into better access for this group. Although down payments in limited-profit housing pose an access barrier, Vienna reduces them by drawing on its powerful policy tool of housing subsidies (i.e. SMART apartments). Municipal and limited-profit housing together still guarantee tenure security, thanks to unlimited contracts, and provide affordable housing by offering the lowest rent. The structural outcome is a split within private rental as well as a split between private and social rental concerning housing conditions. The overrepresentation of low-income groups and non-Austrians in less affordable and less secure sub-segments indicates that the dualisation of housing conditions excludes some of the least well-off. As divides emerge along the lines of residency rather than citizenship, redistribution via social housing and rent control continues to work for sitting tenants; however, this is increasingly not the case for newcomers.

Although conditions have changed and trade-offs are clearly detectable, we argue that Vienna continues its legacy as a *just city* because it continues to take responsibility for affordable and secure housing. As our findings reveal, Vienna's model of *housing for all*, which builds on social housing and rent control in private rental, continues to provide affordable and secure housing for a broad section of the population. Unlike many other European cities, Vienna is characterised by a stable tenure structure, where social housing remains the largest housing segment. However, faced with growing demand, eligibility does not necessarily translate into access and redistribution for everyone in need. The unbalancing of part of the private rental segment threatens the City's redistributive capacity and jeopardises the just housing system of Vienna. In the absence of stricter national rent regulations, only an expanding social housing segment can guarantee the continuation of a just housing system in Vienna.

References

Andersson, R. and Turner, L.M., 2014. Segregation, gentrification, and residualisation: From public housing to market-driven housing allocation in inner city Stockholm. *International Journal of Housing Policy*, 14(1), pp. 3–29.

Emmenegger, P., ed., 2012. *The age of dualization: The changing face of inequality in deindustrializing societies*. New York: Oxford University Press.

Fainstein, S., 2010. *The just city*. Ithaca, NY and London: Cornell University Press.

Hochstenbach, C. and Ronald, R., 2020. The unlikely revival of private renting in Amsterdam: Re-regulating a regulated housing market. *Environment and Planning A*, 52(8), pp. 1622–1642.

Kadi, J., 2015. Recommodifying housing in formerly "Red" Vienna? *Housing, Theory and Society*, 32(3), pp. 247–265.

Kadi, J. and Musterd, S., 2014. Housing for the poor in a neo-liberalising just city: Still affordable, but increasingly inaccessible. *Tijdschrift voor economische en sociale geografie*, 106(3), pp. 246–262.

Kohlbacher, J. and Reeger, U., 2020. Globalization, immigration and ethnic diversity: The exceptional case of Vienna. In: Musterd, S., ed., 2020. *Handbook of urban segregation*. Cheltenham: Edward Elgar Publishing, pp. 101–117.

Lévy-Vroelant, C. and Reinprecht, C., 2014. Housing the poor in Paris and Vienna: The changing understanding of the 'social'. In: Scanlon, K., Whitehead, C. and Fernández Arrigoitia, M., eds., 2014. *Social housing in Europe*. Oxford: John Wiley & Sons, pp. 297–313.

Matznetter, W., 2002. Social housing policy in a conservative welfare state: Austria as an Example. *Urban Studies*, 39(2), pp. 265–282.

Mundt, A., 2018. Privileged but challenged: The state of social housing in Austria in 2018. *Critical Housing Analysis*, 5(1), pp. 12–25.

Mundt, A. and Amann, W., 2010. Indicators of an integrated rental market in Austria. *Housing Finance International*, 25(2), pp. 35–44.

STEP 2025, 2014. *Urban development plan Vienna STEP 2025*. Vienna: Municipal Department 18 (MA 18).

Stephens, M., 2020. How housing systems are changing and why: A critique of Kemeny's theory of housing regimes. *Housing, Theory and Society*, 37(5), pp. 521–547.

Tockner, L., 2017. *Mieten in Österreich und Wien 2008–2016*. Wien: AK Wien.

Van Duijne, R. and Ronald, R., 2018. The unravelling of Amsterdam's unitary rental system. *Journal of Housing and the Built Environment*, 33(4), pp. 633–651.

5 Innovating social housing? Tracing the social in social housing construction

Michael Friesenecker and Katharina Litschauer

Introduction

Since the 1980s, the traditional role of social housing in Europe – which aimed to ensure affordable housing for a broad cross-section of its citizens – has become increasingly threatened by public expenditure pressures, liberalisation and privatisation (Scanlon et al., 2015). The changing economic and political context has forced many countries and cities to adapt their social housing approaches. Some cities and countries have privatised (parts of) their social housing to sitting tenants, such as the UK's Right to Buy programme (ibid); retreated from active housing policies and public financial support, like Berlin (Marquardt and Glaser, 2020); or transformed public social housing into market-based cooperatives, like Stockholm (Andersson and Turner, 2014). Meanwhile, Austria and France actually expanded their social housing sector, but the sector became increasingly fragmented, though the term *social* in social housing remains meaningful (Lévy-Vroelant et al., 2014). Following this diverse landscape, Granath Hansson and Lund (2019, p. 149) claim that, across Europe, social housing has increasingly become a 'floating signifier' without an agreed meaning, though a focus on households with limited financial resources is observable. However, social housing in Vienna contrasts with this narrow definition, as it aims to cater for broad sections of the population and consists of both affordable and high-quality housing.

Against this background, this chapter analyses how social housing construction in Vienna has been adapted in light of a changing urban context and explores how the social in social housing has been redefined since 1990. In doing so, we draw on the concept of 'social innovation', which refers to innovation as the capacity to create and implement new solutions that meet the social needs of social groups or the challenges of society as a whole (BEPA, 2010). Changing housing

DOI: 10.4324/9781003133827-7

needs due to labour market restructuring, immigration, climate and societal change present such challenges (Braga and Palvarini, 2013). This raises the question of how Vienna deals with these challenges and how this in turn re-shapes social housing. Social innovation, as our analytical focus, allows us to explore how social housing is more than the provision of affordable housing for low-income households. It highlights how the social in housing is contested and re-negotiated, rooted in the relations and behaviour of multiple actors across multiple levels. Following Reinprecht (2021), we investigate shifts in the regulatory framework and highlight changes in both the actors' constellations and the prevailing system of norms and values.

Although Vienna retreated from state provision by handing the task of social housing construction to limited-profit housing associations (LPHAs), the City continues to steer new construction by drawing on a specific set of policy instruments and actors. The concept of 'state-directed hybridity' (Mullins et al., 2017) emphasises the decisive role of the state in shaping social agendas of (limited-profit) housing associations and allows for an analysis of the extent to which the City retained its power to actively influence the *social*. As such, we can grasp how policy instruments have reshaped both values and actors' constellations within social innovation.

To evaluate the outcome of social innovation, we draw on Fainstein's (2010) concept of a 'just city' – according to which the status of a just city should be analysed against the core values of equity, diversity and democracy. Each of these three criteria must be present at a minimum level, even though they are in tension with one another and can never all be fully realised. Diversity allows for an analysis of how the City recognises changing and diverse housing needs. Regarding democracy, we investigate the involvement and participation of different actors, in particular, the empowerment of residents to become co-producers rather than mere consumers of their living environment (Moulaert, 2010). Equity focuses on redistributive outcomes and highlights aspects of eligibility, access and affordability. This analytical framework allows us to shed light on how social innovations redefine the *social* in just ways as we assess how trade-offs between equity, diversity and democracy influence the constant re-negotiation of the *social*.

The city's steering role in social housing construction

Social housing has a long tradition in Vienna and is provided by both the municipality and LPHAs. Even from its roots in the era of *Red*

Vienna (1922–1934), Vienna's municipal housing construction aimed to address the housing needs of the time, which were marked by poor housing conditions and the common practise of subletting single beds within the private rental market. Municipal housing provided apartments with lavatories and running water, as well as communal infrastructure, such as schools, libraries, green spaces and common washing and laundry rooms. The aim of providing these central elements was to enhance the living standards of the working class and municipal servants (Lévy-Vroelant and Reinprecht, 2014; Kadi and Suitner, 2019). In a similar vein, the origins of LPHAs lie in the collective, self-managed housing provision of cooperatives, especially after the First World War, as well as employer initiatives to provide decent housing for their staff (Bauer, 2006). After the Second World War, Vienna's focus shifted towards the mass production of housing throughout the 1950s, and improvements in apartment quality throughout the 1960s. These efforts were supported by the introduction of housing subsidies on a national level and the reinstatement of the non-profit housing law. The latter became crucial cornerstones of Austria's post-war housing policy and paved the way for LPHAs (Matznetter, 2002). The 1970s saw the return to greater architectural diversity, higher construction quality and a renewed interest in experimenting with collaborative housing and communal infrastructure. However, this development mainly took place in the limited-profit sector (Schluder, 2005).

After the fall of the Iron Curtain in 1989 and Austria's accession to the European Union, Vienna faced particularly profound political and socio-demographic challenges that also affected social housing provision. After decades of stagnation, population growth increased the demand for housing and brought new challenges in an ever more densely populated city. Without abandoning its core value of providing social housing for many, social-democratic Vienna was forced to adapt its social housing provision as a reaction to new EU budgetary and state aid regulations. Figure 5.1 shows how the construction of social housing by LPHAs already outweighed municipal housing construction throughout the 1990s, whilst the latter ceased completely in 2004 (see Chapter 4 by Litschauer and Friesenecker in this volume). LPHAs became even more important in constructing outsourced public housing as public-private partnerships. Against this context, social housing construction became increasingly characterised as a state-directed hybridity in which the political-administrative apparatus defines its goals, whilst organisational-economic implementation was handed over to the housing associations (Bauer, 2006, p. 24).

Innovating social housing 71

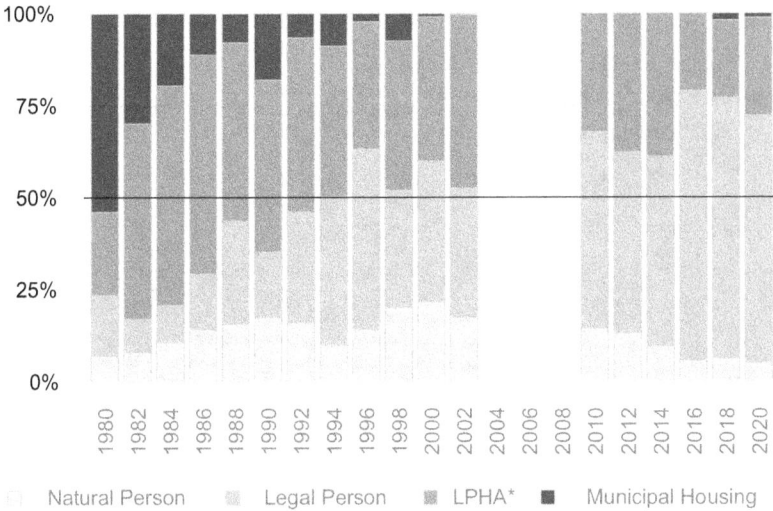

Figure 5.1 Share of building permits for dwellings per developer in Vienna (%), 1980–2020.
Source: STATcube – Statistische Datenbank von STATISTIK AUSTRIA Baumaßnahmenstatistik; Author's own elaboration.
Note: *Limited-profit housing associations. For 1980–2002 building permits for apartments in new buildings plus attics conversions and extensions. For 2003–2009 no data available. For 2010–2020 building permits for dwellings in new buildings only. Figures for 2017–2020 are estimated.

LPHAs are one of the core actors in today's social housing construction and have been regulated by the national Limited-Profit Housing Act since 1978. LPHAs can either be organised as cooperatives, owned by its members or as limited liability corporations. Legally, the distribution of profits is limited to 3.5%, which is why they do not aim at maximising profits. Furthermore, housing associations are obliged to reinvest profits into housing, but in exchange they benefit from tax exemptions. Hence, the core values of these third sector actors are the provision of affordable housing through cost-covering rent and inter-generational housing provision through long-term maintenance and reinvestment into housing (GBV, 2021).

Figure 5.1 highlights the importance of LPHAs in housing construction in relation to commercial developers. Whilst commercial developers were only marginally active until the late 1980s, they became a strong competitor for LPHAs as the municipality progressively retreated from construction. Nevertheless, the City continues to manage

Distribution and Size of Social Housing Premises, Vienna

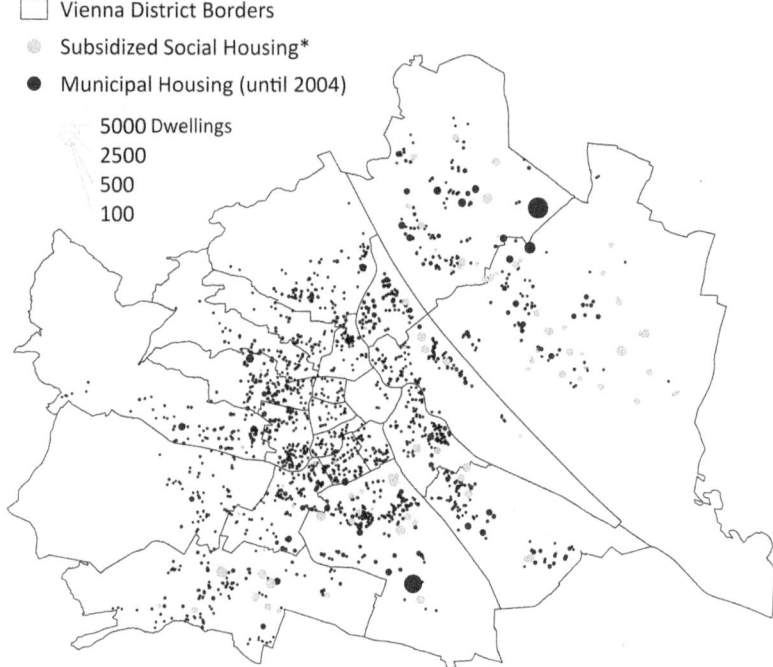

Figure 5.2 Distribution of municipal housing stock and new subsidised housing construction via developer competitions, 2020.

Sources: CC BY 3.0 data.gv.at for municipal housing. For subsidised social housing: Descriptions of developer competitions, Wohnfonds Wien – https://bit.ly/3esbvMQ, Author's own elaboration.

Note: *Output of developer competitions since 1995 and built until 2020; mainly constructed by limited-profit housing associations (LPHA).

its existing municipal housing stock. Figure 5.2 shows that municipal housing and, as far as possible, new subsidised social housing are distributed across the whole city. This is emblematic of Vienna's core values in housing policy: to avoid segregation across the city and provide mixed social housing to a broad section of the population.

As the historical trajectory of social housing provision in Vienna highlights, the core values of the municipality and the LPHAs shape the social in social housing. Nevertheless, in retreating from the construction of municipal housing, the City had to find new ways to secure its core values in social housing construction and sustain limited-profit housing. Albeit in a steering role, the City's approach to influencing the *social* in social housing construction has built on three highly interrelated policy instruments: (1) through an active land banking and zoning policy that guarantees affordable building plots; (2) by subsidising housing construction to ensure low housing costs; and (3) through steering the criteria included in developer competitions to ensure the social orientation and housing quality. We elaborate on each of these below.

The introduction of a City-owned land provision fund in 1985 – today known as the *wohnfonds_wien* (*Housing Fund of Vienna*) – laid the groundwork for Vienna's active land banking policy. As the Executive Councillor for Housing is the president of the fund, the core values of the City's housing policy are clearly reflected in the fund's strategic orientation and objectives. The main objective is central land acquisition to keep land prices low, limit competition between (limited profit) developers and secure land for future urban developments. For the construction of subsidised social housing in recent decades, the fund started to buy land in planned urban development areas from the late 1980s onwards (Schluder, 2005, p. 15). The provision of affordable land is key to (subsidised) social housing as the overall land costs are capped to ensure below-market rents. Nevertheless, from 2008 onwards, the City faced severe challenges in buying up land because commercial developers became a strong competitor and land prices increased (see Figure 5.1). As a consequence, Vienna increased its commitment to an active land banking and zoning policy and introduced a new social housing zoning category in 2018. This applies to large, newly rezoned building plots and demands that at least half of all housing units must be subsidised social housing. For these units, rent caps and a ban on resale apply for the duration of the subsidy (usually 40 years).

While various European countries, such as the Czech Republic, England and Sweden (Scanlon et al., 2015), have shifted their housing subsidies to individual housing allowances at the expense of their social housing supply, Vienna continues to subsidise housing construction. In 2017, for instance, around 50% of expenses were used for new construction, 34% for subsidised renovation and around 16% for housing allowances (Mundt et al., 2018). With the devolution of the centralised Austrian housing subsidy system to the regional level, Vienna – which is both a *Bundesland* and a municipality – became legally responsible for housing subsidies in 1989. The subsidies are mainly financed through a 1% housing tax on wages, which is equally paid by employers and employees, collected at the national level and distributed to the *Bundesländer* (Marquardt and Glaser, 2020). The decentralisation of housing subsidies granted the City of Vienna the legal autonomy to develop subsidy schemes, define target groups and income limits, allocate part of the housing units, and regulate rent for the duration of the subsidy (35–40 years). Hence, housing subsidies allow the City to influence not only affordability (by providing cheap financing and implementing a rent cap), but also to demand certain housing qualities as specified in the subsidy schemes.

In contrast to other European countries, except for Scandinavian welfare regimes (Lévy-Vroelant et al., 2014, p. 285), Austria – but especially Vienna – mainly subsidises the construction of multi-storey rental unit housing. Vienna's bricks-and-mortar subsidies consist largely of loans, which generate a stable stream of revenue for financing future housing construction. Additionally, non-repayable grants contribute to fostering (ecological) housing qualities. In practice, housing subsidies are mostly dispersed to LPHAs, while commercial developers also rarely construct subsidised (social) housing. It is important to note that rent regulations apply for the duration of the subsidy loan; hence private subsidised housing can only temporarily be considered social housing. In contrast, LPHAs are only allowed to charge cost-covering rent, implying that the rent must be lowered substantially after subsidy loans are paid back (Marquardt and Glaser, 2020). Hence, LPHAs are legally obliged to construct permanent social housing. Furthermore, profits must be re-invested in renovation or new constructions, thereby providing affordable, high-quality housing and securing social housing in the long run.

Moreover, the major tool that allows the City to shape the social orientation of subsidised housing is its developer competitions, organised by the *wohnfonds_wien*. Introduced in 1995 as an architectural and urban design competitive tender procedure, it is the main tool to allocate City-owned building plots and housing subsidies. These apply to large development projects (more than 500 units since 2016) on City-owned land and/or projects that receive housing subsidies. Smaller projects are evaluated by a property advisory board. As well as LPHAs, commercial developers are also allowed to take part in these competitions. While the city administration disburses the subsidy, the tendering process is implemented by the *wohnfonds_wien*. Competitions demand that developers team up with architects, landscape architects and other experts, and competition calls often include specific themes. Through a multi-disciplinary jury, consisting of experts in architecture, urban design, ecology, etc., as well as representatives of the districts, the city administration and *wohnfonds_wien* award the best projects. The assessment follows economic, architectural, ecological criteria and, since 2009, the criterion of *social sustainability*. These criteria are politically determined which explains why they go beyond pure economic aspects. Furthermore, as outlined above, rent in newly constructed, subsidised social housing is capped. Therefore, projects must fulfil the requirement of providing affordable housing, while the competitive tendering procedure demands innovative, high-quality housing solutions. In this sense, developer competitions are understood by the administration as a steering instrument that ensures high-quality housing and fosters social innovation.

Innovating social housing construction via developer competitions in just ways?

After outlining how Vienna continues to shape social housing construction by drawing on different policy instruments, this section analyses how the *social* in social housing has been adapted and innovated through developer competitions. We trace how these social innovations were articulated in response to urban challenges and analyse them with regard to trade-offs between equity, diversity and democracy. First, we discuss how housing needs have been recognised in developer competitions and how this has influenced housing outcomes with regard to diversity and equity. Second, we analyse how the tendering procedure has been innovated, incorporating participatory elements for residents, and how this has improved democracy.

Innovating high-quality, yet affordable social housing

After being introduced in 1995, developer competitions were based on specific themes and used by the administration as the main tool to influence the orientation of new social housing construction. In his evaluation of developer competitions, Liske (2008) concludes that, until 2008, more than half of the competitions had been theme-oriented, focusing on ecological and social aspects. As Vienna committed itself to climate mitigation policies during the 1990s, ecological issues were also taken up in developer competition calls. While passive housing standards and wood construction remained experimental, low-energy buildings, ecological building site management and ventilation systems for reducing the heating demands became general standards in (social) housing construction. This mainstreaming of high ecological standards became possible because the criteria of architecture, economy and ecology were treated as equally important in the evaluation procedure (Schluder, 2005; Liske, 2008).

At the beginning of the 21st century, socio-demographic changes and migration became more pronounced. The City of Vienna increasingly recognised the housing needs of disadvantaged groups in urban planning, including women, migrants, young and elderly people, as well as disabled persons (MA18, 2005). Subsequently, topics of intercultural, inter-generational and female-orientated living, or housing solutions for single adults and affordable housing for younger generations were taken up as special themes in the competition calls (Reven-Holzmann, 2019). These themed tenders led to the provision of diverse apartment layouts, ranging mostly in size and the numbers of rooms, accommodating different housing needs. This is a development that should not be underestimated as, in the 1990s, usually only one type of ground floor plan for the nuclear family had been foreseen (Schluder, 2005).

Following these experiences, the design of the tendering procedure was modified in 2009 to explicitly integrate the housing needs of different social groups, while adding *social sustainability* as a fourth evaluation criterion. This criterion emphasises the usability of apartments, buildings and (semi-)public spaces in everyday life, but also fostering collaborative living and serving diverse housing needs. Developer competitions initially encouraged the provision of private free space in the form of gardens, loggias and balconies, and from 2009 onwards barrier-free designs became standard (Reven-Holzmann, 2019). Most importantly, following the legacy of the Red Vienna era, the provision of communal spaces was (re)emphasised along with the introduction of social sustainability. Communal spaces vary from project to project, including fitness rooms, swimming pools or multipurpose rooms for birthday celebrations or family gatherings, but the most requested communal spaces are still laundry rooms (Reven-Holzmann, 2019). Often not realised due to budget restrictions in projects of the 1990s and 2000s (Schluder, 2005), recent competitions have highlighted the importance and accessibility of green and open spaces for different user groups and ages, including semi-public spaces, like rooftops. Therefore, special emphasis is placed on the qualities of playgrounds and parks, including urban gardening infrastructure, which gained momentum in recent years.

However, some local experts began to address an increasing trade-off between improved housing quality and affordability. Especially after the mid-2000s, in the context of renewed population growth and price increases in the construction sector, improved building standards led to higher costs for tenants, especially regarding capital contributions (Liske, 2008). The global financial crisis of 2008 further aggravated the situation as real estate became attractive for commercial developers and affordable building plots scarce for LPHAs. In light of these developments, affordability became the dominant theme and calls for tender progressively emphasised housing costs.

A tendering competition in 2012 saw a first experimental attempt to cap construction costs, down-payments and rent levels, by limiting floor size (Reven-Holzmann, 2019). Following its success, this experiment was further mainstreamed to the *SMART Housing Program* (Wohnfonds Wien, 2019). The program aims at providing compact apartments (40–100 m^2, depending on family size) with capped down-payments when signing the contract, ranging from 2,400 to 6,000 EUR (2019). Down-payments can be further reduced with means-tested loans provided by the City, and the allocation of SMART apartments is more strictly regulated (for details on down-payments and allocation criteria, see Chapter 4 by Litschauer and Friesenecker in this volume). From 2012 onwards, the tendering process required that one-third of all new subsidised housing units be built as *SMART* units, and this was extended to one half in 2019 (Wohnfonds Wien, 2019). In addition, projects experimented tentatively with the provision of other housing forms, such as subsidised dormitories, for example, in the form of night shelters for the homeless, or starter apartments as part of the *Housing First* approach (Reven-Holzmann, 2019).

Hence, developer competitions were adapted to ensure more equitable outcomes, while continuing to promote diversity and high housing quality. Subsidising LPHAs as hybrid actors allowed the City to respond to environmental and socio-demographic challenges, adopt norms and values accordingly, and enhance diversity in social housing. It has also allowed them to secure more equitable outcomes in the long run through limited-profit housing with the cost-covering principle in rent-setting and the requirement to reinvest profits into housing continue after the funding period. The introduction of SMART apartments shows that the City actively intervenes and balances the trade-off between equity and diversity. Although this trade-off between high quality, diversity and affordability exists in new (social) housing, the City of Vienna continues to acknowledge the central role of housing for social cohesion, even in the light of pronounced urban challenges.

Innovation by enhancing participation opportunities

Vienna has traditionally been characterised by a *top-down* governing style, but in recent decades the City has enabled more opportunities for participation at the neighbourhood level (see Chapter 3 by Ahn and Mocca in this volume). Similarly, the participation of residents in planning and designing the living environment in (social) housing construction has traditionally been quite limited. However, with the introduction of social sustainability in 2009, the city administration increasingly promoted new modes of participation in developer competitions that aim at fostering collaborative housing.

Initially, the provision of communal rooms and green spaces did not result in higher usage rates, which is why issues of appropriation and self-management through residents became more central in developer competitions (Reven-Holzmann, 2019). The main response to this challenge was the introduction of so-called settlement management processes, which focus on tenants' participation after they move in. Equipped with a dedicated budget, consultants became part of interdisciplinary project teams to facilitate and mediate community building and self-organisation. Since that time, it has become standard not to fully equip and plan every community room in detail, but to leave it to tenants to clarify use concepts during the settlement process and to self-organise (parts of) the maintenance of community infrastructure. This should at least serve 'the committed residents' who are willing to co-design the use of community rooms according to their needs (Reven-Holzmann, 2019, p. 86). Vienna's approach to social housing construction, therefore, not only aims to address diversity by recognising diverse housing needs, but also enhances aspects of democracy by giving tenants the opportunity to participate (ibid.). Yet, participation is limited, as projects that allow for co-planning the apartment (layout) are rarely implemented. In general, social housing construction is still mainly characterised by top-down planning decisions to serve different needs in the long run.

With regard to fostering participation, but also in relation to serving diverse housing needs, Vienna's social housing approach also started to subsidise co-housing projects (*Bau- und Wohngruppen*) more prominently since 2009. These projects are characterised by a self-determined approach of associations of citizens that initiate, plan and (co-)develop collaborative housing for self-use and communitarian services. Following a commissioned study, which explored the regulatory context and legal obstacles for co-housing in Vienna, procedures to allocate land to co-housing projects in urban development areas were introduced (Temel et al., 2009, p. 51). In 2012, *wohnfonds_wien* introduced specific co-housing competitions where land was allocated to co-housing projects. The City subsidised co-housing in order to establish diversity at the neighbourhood level, provide common spaces open to other residents of the neighbourhood and to foster vibrant neighbourhoods (Reven-Holzmann, 2019).

Nevertheless, tenants in co-housing are usually more homogenous in socio-economic and socio-demographic terms than tenants in mainstream social housing. Following Temel et al. (2009), it is largely the higher educated groups with sufficient financial and time resources who are able to participate in and finance the planning process of such projects. Compared to the standard model of subsidised social housing built by limited-profit housing association, the provision of subsidised co-housing is very limited in scope (Gruber and Lang, 2018). Hence, their effect on the trade-off between equity and democracy is limited, but mostly better-off individuals benefit from this new mode of (social) housing construction. Nonetheless, these projects shape living conditions in the neighbourhood and influence prevailing social norms and existing relations between residents.

Conclusions

Given the vast but variegated transformations of social housing across Europe since the 1980s, this chapter aimed to fill the floating signifier on how the *social* is articulated in Vienna's social housing construction. Contrary to recent trends that restrict social housing to residents with limited financial resources (Granath Hansson and Lund, 2019), this chapter emphasises how Vienna's approach to social housing construction goes beyond simply producing affordable housing for low-income households. Rooted in the social-democratic history of the City of Vienna, social housing construction continues to pursue its core values: avoiding segregation and emphasising the social aspects of housing for the many. New social housing provides affordable, high-quality housing to a broad section of society, whilst also shaping the way people live together.

Unlike many other cities and countries that retrenched from state support for social housing, Vienna continued to actively influence prevailing norms, values and outcomes in social housing construction. With the interplay of land market intervention, housing construction subsidies and the specific use of developer competitions, Vienna retained its capacity to shape the *social* in social housing through a steering role. This renewed approach, which can be characterised as 'state-directed hybridity' (Mullins et al., 2017), depends on a specific actor's constellation in which LPHAs play a key role. Regulated at the national level, LPHAs share the City's values regarding social housing and, as actors of the third sector, are able to provide high-quality and affordable housing through cost-covering rent and the obligation to reinvest profits.

A core instrument in addressing urban challenges and adapting social housing construction accordingly is the specific use of developer competitions. As projects must fulfil the requirements of affordable housing through rent caps, developer competitions demand innovative, high-quality housing solutions to address urban challenges. Whilst social housing construction specifically responded to ecological challenges during the 1990s, it increasingly addressed diverse housing needs and focused on solutions for socio-demographic changes. This was further mainstreamed by introducing social sustainability as a new criterion in developer competitions in 2009, thereby enhancing diversity and democracy by influencing housing outcomes as well as residents' relations. Faced with affordability challenges, the City introduced SMART apartments to enhance equity. Moreover, by fostering different modes of participation, the City increasingly emphasised aspects of social cohesion within its social housing approach. This implies shifts in prevailing values and indicates redefinitions of the *social* in social housing.

Finally, through the lens of the *just city* (Fainstein, 2010), we assessed the outcomes of these redefinitions with regard to trade-offs between equity, diversity and democracy. Such trade-offs always exist in (social) housing and are also detectable in Vienna's approach. Since newly constructed housing is more expensive than the existing (social) housing stock, achieving equitable outcomes remains a challenge. However, by targeting the existing municipal housing stock at relatively disadvantaged groups (see Chapter 4 by Litschauer and Friesenecker), the City is able to buffer the trade-off with regard to equity in newly constructed social housing. By relying on limited profit housing, Vienna is additionally able to shape future housing in terms of enhancing the recognition of diverse housing needs and the limited incorporation of more participatory practices.

Social housing in Vienna has always been about more than providing affordable housing, also encompassing the aim of social cohesion. As the analysis of social innovation of developer competitions shows, this continues to the present day. In the European context, Vienna leads the way in developing new solutions in urban housing systems. Social housing is – and should be – about more than just affordable housing, since housing is not only an economic question but a social one, and justice refers to more than only economic redistribution.

References

Andersson, R., and Turner, M. L., 2014. Segregation, gentrification, and residualisation: from public housing to market-driven housing allocation in inner city Stockholm. *International Journal of Housing Policy*, 14(1), pp. 3–29.

Bauer, E., 2006. Gemeinnütziger Wohnbau in Österreich. Zu Geschichte, Funktion und künftiger Perspektive. *Kurswechsel*, 3, pp. 20–27.
BEPA (Bureau of European Policy Advisors), 2011. *Empowering people, driving change: Social innovation in the European Union*.
Braga, M. and Palvarini, P., 2013. *Social housing in the EU*. Policy Department A: Economic and Scientific Policy, European Parliament (Brussels).
Fainstein, S., 2010. *The just city*. Ithaca, NY: Cornell University Press.
GBV, 2021. *Leitbild der Gemeinnützigen*. Available at: https://bit.ly/3u7dv3e [Accessed 28 March 2021].
Granath Hansson, A. and Lundgren, B., 2019. Defining social housing: A discussion on the suitable criteria. *Housing, Theory and Society*, 36(2), pp. 149–166. https://bit.ly/2YAUqg4
Gruber, E. and Lang, R., 2018. Collaborative housing models in Vienna through the lens of social innovation. In: Van Bortel, G., Gruis, V., Nieuwenhuijzen, J. and Pluijmers, B., eds., 2018. *Affordable housing governance and finance innovations, partnerships and comparative perspectives*. Abingdon and New York: Routledge, pp. 42–58.
Kadi, J. and Suitner, J., 2019. Red Vienna, 1919–1934. In: Orum, A.M., ed., 2019. *The Wiley Blackwell encyclopedia of urban and regional studies*, pp. 1–5. https://bit.ly/3fxr600
Lévy-Vroelant, C. and Reinprecht, C., 2014. Housing the poor in Paris and Vienna: The changing understanding of 'the social'. In: Scanlon, K., Whitehead, C. and Fernandez Arrigoitia, M., eds., 2014. *Social housing in Europe*. Oxford: Wiley-Blackwell, pp. 297–314.
Lévy-Vroelant, C., Reinprecht, C., Robertson, D. and Wassenberg, F., 2014. Learning from history: Path dependency and change in the social housing sectors of Austria, France, the Netherlands and Scotland, 1889–2013. In: Scanlon, K. and Fernandez Arrigoitia, M., eds., 2014. *Social housing in Europe*. Oxford: Wiley-Blackwell, pp. 277–296.
Liske, H., 2008. *Der "Bauträgerwettbewerb" als Instrument des geförderten sozialen Wohnbaus in Wien – verfahrenstechnische und inhaltliche Evaluierung*. [pdf] Available at: https://bit.ly/2PHcyjn [Accessed 01 April 2021]
MA18, 2005. *Stadtentwicklungsplan 2005. Short Report*. [pdf] Available at: https://bit.ly/3fxqlnC [Accessed 01 April 2021].
Marquardt, S. and Glaser, D., 2020. How much state and how much market? Comparing social housing in Berlin and Vienna. *German Politics*, ahead-of-print, pp. 1–20.
Matznetter, W., 2002. Social housing policy in a conservative welfare state: Austria as an example. *Urban Studies*, 39(2), pp. 265–282.
Moulaert, F., 2010. Social innovation and community development. Concepts, theories and challenges. In: Moulaert, F., Swyngedouw, E., Martinelli, F. and Gonzalez, S., eds., 2010. *Can neighbourhoods save the city? Community development and social innovation*. London: Routledge, pp. 20–32.
Mullins, D., Milligan, V. and Nieboer, N., 2017. State directed hybridity? – The relationship between non-profit housing organisations and the state in three national contexts. *Housing Studies*, 33(4), pp. 565–588.

Mundt, A., Komendantova, N. and Amann, W., 2018. *Berichtsstandard Wohnbauförderung 2018*. [online] Available at: https://bit.ly/3rHMDp9 [Accessed 01 April 2021].

Reinprecht, C., 2021. The local dimension of housing policies. In: Kazepov, Y., Barberis, Mocca, E. and Cucca, R., eds., 2021. *Handbook on urban social policy. International perspectives on multilevel governance and local welfare*. Cheltenham: Edward Elgar. Forthcoming.

Reven-Holzmann, A., 2019. *10 Jahre "Soziale Nachhaltigkeit". Bestandsaufnahme und Ausblick*. [pdf] Available at: https://bit.ly/3do29RJ [Accessed 01 April 2021].

Scanlon, K., Fernández Arrigoitia, M. and Whitehead, C.M.E., 2015. Social housing in Europe. *European Policy Analysis*, 17, pp. 1–12.

Schluder, M., 2005. *10 Jahre Bauträgerwettbewerb. Veränderungen im Wohnbau*. [online] Available at: https://bit.ly/3meAWF9 [Accessed 01 April 2021].

Temel, R., Lorbek, M., Ptaszyńska, A. and Wittinger, D., 2009. *Baugemeinschaften in Wien: Endbericht 1- Potenzialabschätzung und Rahmenbedingungen*. [online] Available at: https://bit.ly/3uffrXQ [Accessed 01 April 2021].

Wohnfonds Wien, 2019. *SMART-wohnen*. [pdf] Available at: https://bit.ly/3wdd6ln [Accessed March 28 2021].

Part III
Labour market

6 Between protection and activation

Shifting institutional arrangements and 'ambivalent' labour market policies in Vienna

Byeongsun Ahn and Yuri Kazepov

Introduction

In the international debate, Austria has always been defined as a corporatist welfare model, characterised by a high degree of political cooperation and policy concertation between different interest groups (Österle and Heitzmann, 2020). In this 'partnership', the interest intermediation between political parties and the social 'partners' representing employees (the Chamber of Labour/the Federation of the Trade Union), and employers (the Economic Chamber/the Federation of Austrian Industries) were central to the formulation and implementation of economic and social policies based on a consensus-building model. Between 1957 and 1998, the core organisation of this partnership was the *Parity Commission*, an informal policy-making body comprising the four major social partners and members of the government (Lewis, 2002). Its subcommittees (on international affairs, economic and social affairs, prices and wages) and working parties delivered unanimous policy recommendations to the commission, around which the federal government formulated policies in conformity with the interests of the social partners[1] (Gilbert, 1987). This recognition of their social role and the strong coordination led to relative consistency and stability in federal labour market policies, giving the social partners a quasi-monopoly in the corporatist policy-making process (Tálos and Hinterseer, 2019), also influencing the redistributive process.

However, in line with international trends (Natali et al., 2018), the bargaining power of the social partners have diminished in recent decades. This has been exacerbated, especially under the two conservative-right-wing federal governments (2000–2007/2017–2019) that initiated restructuring processes in the Austrian welfare system

DOI: 10.4324/9781003133827-9

(Tálos and Hinterseer, 2019). Despite the anti-welfare rhetoric at the federal level, however, the path-dependent effects of the institutional evolution at the regional level have led to particular redistributive outcomes in Vienna. The institutional capacity of Vienna – being simultaneously a *Bundesland* and a *municipality* – and the longevity of the Socialist Democrats in power (see Chapter 2 by Mocca et al. in this volume) allowed the local government to actively formulate its own economic and social policies beyond the shifting priorities of the federal government. This particular outcome owes much to the decentralisation process of labour market policies that rescaled important responsibilities to the city level in the early 1990s, which empowered the local authority to innovate and develop a localised welfare model that maintained its inclusive characteristics. Contrary to centralised welfare services that remain strong in other European cities, for example in France (*Revenu de solidarité active*), Germany (*Hartz IV*), or the United Kingdom (*Job Seekers Allowance*), Vienna's new-found regulatory autonomy has, on the one hand, engendered new solutions to the structural problems of its local labour market, and on the other hand, allowed for the federal welfare retrenchment and restructuring in a more inclusive way.

The structural context of institutional change

Since the mid-1970s, the decline of the city's traditional manufacturing activities – both in terms of workplaces (1973/1981: −17.9%) and employment (1973/1981: −19.4%) – interrupted the employment growth that had characterised the post-war economic boom. The city's shrinking population (1971/1981: −5.5%) – due to the end of the guest-worker recruitment programme, a low birth rate, aging population and the growing trend towards suburbanisation – further reinforced this trend. This situation was exacerbated by a lack of sectoral mobility for the displaced workers and the vulnerability of small- and medium-sized businesses vis-à-vis processes of economic restructuring and international competition. The joint effect of these trends brought about a myriad of new urban challenges. In this context, the development of active labour market policies and that of business investment programmes represented the main direct and indirect employment strategies. However, the conflict between the social partners throughout the 1980s and the lack of formal competence for policy formulation at the city level limited the ability to diversify Vienna's urban economy (Lechner et al., 2017). Simultaneously, the rapid expansion of the tertiary sector (e.g. in financial, insurance, and business services, and personal, social and public services) only partially compensated for job losses. This, in turn, hindered labour market reintegration of the displaced manufacturing workers into the expanding tertiary sector (for more on the structural shift in the Viennese economy during this period, see Chapter 7 by Riederer et al. in this volume).

As the unfavourable labour market situation continued in the 1980s – both regionally and nationally – attempts by the federal government to reshape access to welfare for the unemployed accelerated in two directions: (a) the retrenchment of the unemployment insurance scheme at the federal level; and (b) the decentralisation of active labour market policies to the regional level. Of course, the shift towards supply-side economics and the rescaling of the public employment service were widely observed elsewhere in this period. In contrast to the workfarist reforms in the Anglo-Saxon context, however, the high level of regulatory autonomy gained in Vienna enabled the city administration to institutionalise the welfare system, proving resilient to the shifting external environments. The emergence of new forms of governance in the ensuing decade allowed Vienna to provide demand-oriented services to those who were increasingly excluded from the retreating social protection system at the federal level. This outcome owes much to the interdependent institutional settings, featuring a high degree of complementarity between regional institutions, enabling the city administration to mobilise effectively against restrictive reform strategies formulated by the federal government.

Pathway to regionalised active labour market policies (ALMPs) in Vienna

In the mid-1980s, with the end of full employment in a time of global and national upturn in growth, a new political narrative around the unfavourable labour market situation emerged at the federal level. The new discourse portrayed structural unemployment as a lack of individual willingness, on the one hand, and a disparity between 'search' and 'matching', on the other hand (Tálos, 1987). As the focus of federal employment strategies shifted from economic policies to supply-side fiscal measures and restrictive budgetary policies, the relative importance of passive policies diminished, which in turn facilitated more experimental ALMPs. Employment action plans in the mid-1980s, namely *Aktion 8,000*, first introduced new regulatory principles and mechanisms for labour market reintegration of emerging vulnerable groups (e.g. youth, elderly and the long-term unemployed), through self-employment, community projects and social enterprises. Similar to employment schemes in other Western European countries at the time (Bonoli, 2010), these were aimed at creating jobs and subsidising costs in the secondary labour market, combined with new skills training. The success of these experimental programmes – creating around 11,500 jobs nationally between 1983 and 1995 (Lechner et al., 2017) – initiated debates on the efficacy of the existing federal labour market administration, *Arbeitsmarktverwaltung* (AMV), which had attracted criticism for its bureaucratic management that had so far limited participation of regional actors, social partners,[2] employers and private initiatives in the formulation of ALMPs.

In light of this, a semi-autonomous public employment service, *Arbeitsmarktservice* (AMS), was founded in 1994 by the federal government which, for the first time, rescaled the authority to implement labour market policies down to the regional level (*Bundesland*). The decentralisation and liberalisation of employment services to a diverse range of local actors allowed some level of regional flexibility to implement the employment objectives and strategies that had been formulated at the ministerial level. The federal AMS office, however, retained a top-down management structure and set qualitative and quantitative targets for their regional branches. This aimed to maintain a coherent employment policy framework between the federal and regional levels (Biffl, 1998). Despite the greater decision-making authority within the regional AMS branches, local governments could not autonomously formulate active labour market programmes to fit local needs and challenges. For this reason, Vienna initiated a regional employment service that was directly organised by the city administration (Atzmüller, 2009). As a result, the Vienna Employment Promotion Fund, *Wiener ArbeitnehmerInnen Förderungsfonds* (WAFF), was founded in 1995 as an initiative of the Federation of the Trade Union and the Chamber of Labour. This marked a path shaping moment for Vienna's localised ALMP system, featuring strong coordination and complementarity between the AMS Vienna, WAFF, and the social partners within both organisations. Since then, their institutional complementarity enhanced not only the policy capacity of each organisation, but also mutually compensated for their respective deficiencies: the operational ability of the AMS Vienna is limited to supervision of ALMPs for, and transfer payments to, 'registered' unemployed persons, whereas WAFF's vocational reorientation mainly aids those who are in employment. This supplementary form of complementarity that 'provides a missing ingredient' (Deeg, 2007) to one another has been key for the City's effective policy responses, especially when the regulative framework at the federal level was absent – or restrictive.

Between protection and activation 89

Simultaneously, Austria's accession to the European Union in 1995 provided Vienna with a new opportunity to expand its ALMPs and diversify its policy outreach. The new multilevel governance setting promoted by the EU increased the City's institutional capacity, facilitated by greater responsibilities and resources, to respond to local labour market challenges more effectively. In the following year, the European Employment Strategy set new economic objectives that foresaw the development of a *National Action Plan* in 1998 and of *Territorial Employment Pacts* at the regional level in 1999. The latter aimed at translating the broader macroeconomic European objectives into more specific targets. The Lisbon and Stockholm strategies by the European Council identified, for instance, specific employment targets for disadvantaged social groups (at least 60% for women; 50% for those aged 55–64; and 70% in total). In contrast to other European countries, the regional *Territorial Employment Pacts* in Austria were introduced by the federal government as an instrument for implementing the National Action Plan by enhancing the existing policy coordination between regional stakeholders in terms of policy design and fiscal management (Huber, 2004). By organising the pacts at the level of *Bundesländer*, at which necessary resources and substantial decision-making power are available, the Austrian *National Action Plan* foresaw greater autonomy for regional governments to formulate and implement localised employment policies, in accordance with a federal framework (Campbell, 2000). This led to a new mode of governance, based on collaborative policy making between the AMS Vienna and WAFF, whereby the regionalised federal employment service and the City's own employment fund was able to co-design innovative and needs-oriented policy measures for specific social groups. Following the *Territorial Employment Pact – Vienna*, the financial resources for activation measures at the City level made exponential growth, from 436,000 EUR in 1997 to 49 million EUR in 1999, financially supporting almost 10,000 people. The administrative capacity of WAFF to deliver services beyond the traditional welfare recipients enabled the expansion and diversification of activation and employment measures, not only in traditional skills training programmes (2,776; 13 million EUR), but also in wage subsidies (3,275; 14 million EUR), outplacement services (1,832; 11 million EUR), and employment in the secondary market (446; 5 million EUR) (Leitner et al., 2003). This structure was particularly effective in retaining employment of those in subsidised jobs, including some 70% who remained active in the labour market a year after the end of the programme (Leitner et al., 2003).

In sum, the capacity building of regional actors in the early 1990s characterised the innovative aspect of the City's active labour market policy system. The financial and political autonomy of the regional institutions enabled the City of Vienna to formulate and implement active labour market policies beyond the conventional skills training and job matching measures, especially for those who were excluded from the federal social safety net. However, this faced new challenges between 2000 and 2006 during the conservative-right-wing federal government amid the growing 'work-first' approach to unemployment, and, more recently, between 2017 and 2019. At the City level, however, the workfarist attempt to roll back the redistributive policies and dismantle its fundamental structure was hindered by the strong veto opportunity of regional actors against such reforms, despite incremental changes.

Localised outcomes of federal welfare retrenchment

At the federal level, the late-1980s expansion of labour market protection and unemployment insurance-based benefits ended with the amendment of the *Unemployment Insurance Act* in 1993. The amendment foresaw limited access to benefits and coincided with the expansion of ALMPs and the decentralisation of public employment services to the regional level (Obinger and Tálos, 2006). A shift towards a more restrictive welfare state not only made access to unemployment benefit and assistance more difficult, by creating an institutionally structured downwards mobility path (see Figure 6.1). There was a decrease in the net replacement rates from unemployment benefits (from 57% of the monthly net income in 1993 to 56% 1995) and unemployment assistance (from 95% of the previously paid benefit to 92% in 1990), and more restrictive eligibility criteria were introduced (e.g. a longer minimum contribution period from 20 to 26 weeks in 1995 and additional sanctions in instances where individuals refused job offers). This trend was exacerbated under the conservative-right-wing federal government between 2000 and 2006, who introduced an extension to the minimum contribution period required before receiving unemployment benefits to 28 weeks and the reduction of the net replacement rate of unemployment assistance to its current rate (55%).

Efforts to decrease the number of benefit recipients were accompanied by quantitative targets for the reduction of long-term unemployment and increased participation in activation programmes set by the European Employment Strategy. In 2004, a reform lifted the protection of benefit recipients, obliging them to take up jobs even if

Between protection and activation 91

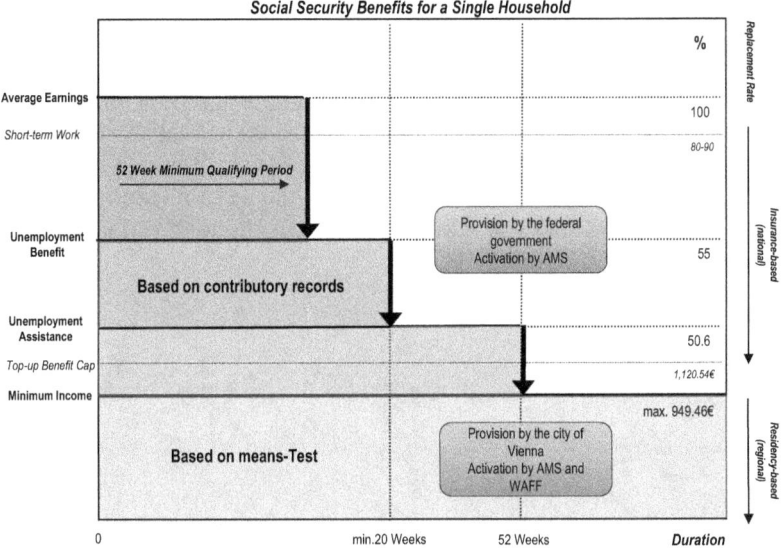

Figure 6.1 Access to unemployment insurance in Austria and Vienna, 2021.
Source: Own Calculation based on Federal Ministry of Social Affairs, Health, Care and Consumer Protection; Public Employment Service Austria.

they mismatched their qualifications during the benefit period.[3] Violations of such rules would imply sanctions, such as the temporary suspension of the benefit – first for six weeks, and then for eight weeks. This reform also made recipients ineligible for further transfer payments if they failed to attend meetings with street-level bureaucrats, as such actions were deemed to indicate an unwillingness to work and the reasonableness of their future employment. During this period, the influence of the Chamber of Labour and the Federation of Trade Unions on the management board of the AMS diminished, and more decisions were made by majority rule rather than full consensus (Tálos and Hinterseer, 2019). The pace and extent of liberalisation was less pronounced in Austria than in other Western European countries, such as Denmark, Germany, and the United Kingdom (Weishaupt, 2011), and was accompanied by a growing share of activation programmes in overall federal spending on labour market policies: from 18% in 2000 to 32% in 2004. This growth was particularly visible in 'activating' financial incentives both to firms and the unemployed (130 million EUR in 2000; 747 million EUR in 2004) that were aimed at increasing the participation of unemployed people below the age of 25 and above 50 in qualification and employment programmes (Obinger and Tálos, 2006). Despite these growing financial efforts, however, the new policy orientation shows a paradigm shift and a trade-off, fostering short-term, 'quick re-entry' labour promotion against labour protection. Whilst ALMPs continued to rise during the conservative-right-wing coalition, they did not target the specific needs of different vulnerable groups on the labour market, undermining the possibility of matching the changing dynamics of labour demand in the long run (Lutz and Mahringer, 2007; Figure 6.2).

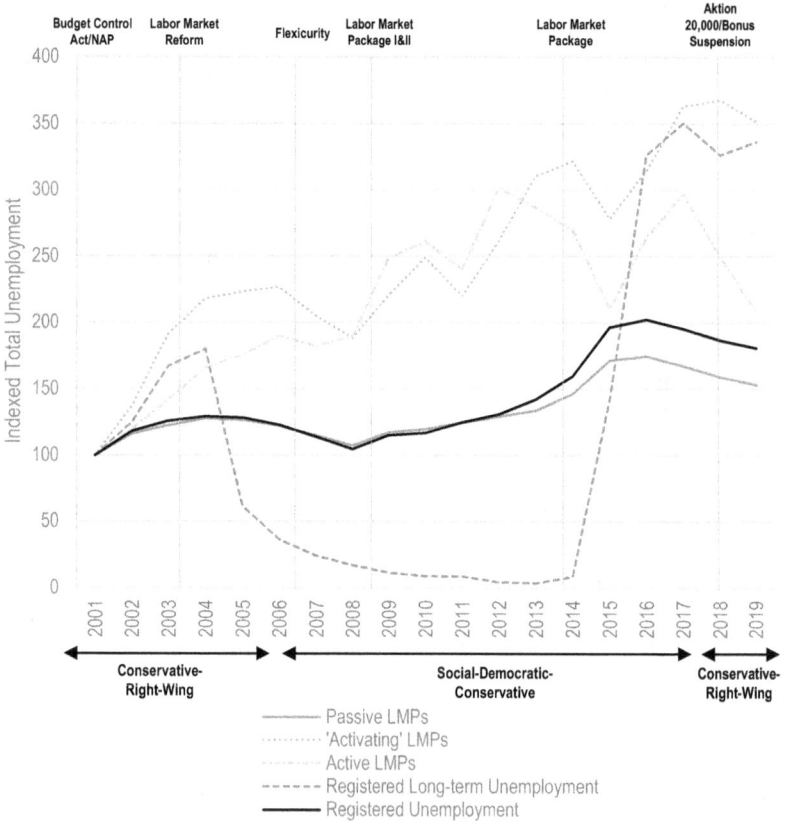

Figure 6.2 Indexed growth of active and passive LMPs in Vienna, 2001–2019 (2001=100).

Source: Public Employment Service Austria, Author's own elaboration.

At the City level, this paradigm shift in the federal welfare system had a direct impact on the types of employment measures that were provided by the AMS Vienna. The restructuring of unemployment insurance produced a growing number of 'activating' financial incentives, and a doubling of training- and old age part-time subsidy recipients in the second year of the first conservative-right-wing federal government (5,124 in 2000; 10,288 in 2001). Since the 2000s, the share of 'activating' measures gradually increased from 8% of all unemployment-related benefit recipients in 1999 (5,124) to 23% in 2006 (23,343). The growth in part-time work subsidies for older workers has been especially high, which together with training subsidies and subsistence allowances, still account for the largest proportion of the 'activating' financial incentives spent to this day (35% in 2001; 29% in 2019). The impact of the growing 'activating' measures was mostly visible in the decline of long-time unemployment, especially in those over the age of 50. This trend reversed with new labour market reforms under the liberal-conservative federal government in 2015, which reoriented the employment strategies. The shifting focus of the federal employment strategies began to prioritise direct job-creation in community projects and social enterprises and offered financial incentives to firms that hired senior and long-term benefit recipients. This lowered the overall number of benefits recipients and increased that of the older and long-term unemployed in the secondary labour market.[4]

These developments ended under the second conservative-right-wing federal government in January 2018. Between 2017 and 2019, retrenchment at the federal level presented further challenges for the City's level of freedom in formulating localised ALMPs beyond the policy priorities of the federal government. One of the immediate impacts on labour force participation was the growth of long-term unemployment amongst those over the age of 55 and those who had not benefited from the favourable labour market situation that began in 2017. Contrary to the restrictive reforms of unemployment insurance in the 2000s, the reform proposals made by the second conservative-right-wing coalition aimed at eliminating unemployment assistance and at centralising the regional means-tested minimum income scheme. However, with the collapse of the federal government in 2019, a number of controversial reform proposals were revaluated, some of which were cancelled, including the abolition of unemployment assistance. Similar to Germany's *Hartz IV* Reform in 2005, it would have put those with limited social insurance contributions and an income below a given threshold directly under a new centralised minimum income scheme. The restructuring of the federal unemployment insurance is now suspended, and Vienna continues to provide a residency-based means-tested minimum income.

Whilst the contribution-based service provision of the AMS Vienna has been – and continues to be – susceptible to shifting policy priorities at the federal level, the localised welfare system based on the City's own redistributive institutions has provided Vienna with greater capacity to broaden its policy outreach. Despite the declining traditional corporatist welfare model during the two conservative-right-wing federal governments, the social partners within the AMS Vienna and WAFF retained relative autonomy in formulating and implementing employment and social policies. In contrast to the move towards tightening access and cutting benefits at the federal level, their institutional complementarity allowed the city administration to expand the boundaries of social protection and inclusion. For example, before the federal minimum income scheme was implemented in 2010, recipients of the regional social benefit were excluded from the activation programmes provided by the AMS, as these were – and continue to be – limited to recipients of unemployment insurance-based benefits. In 2009, a joint pilot project, *Step2Job*, from AMS Vienna and WAFF, co-financed by the European Social Fund, was launched to integrate regional social assistance recipients between the age of 21 and 64 into the activation programmes of the AMS. In coordination with the municipal social welfare office, the pilot gave 800 'top-up' income recipients access to personalised employment services; of these, 26% entered into employment with full compulsory insurance, and 44% into temporary employment. To date, the social benefit recipients were excluded from the federal welfare programmes because of a lack of contributory records. Following its expansion, the City of Vienna was able to implement more inclusive employment services for a broader group of vulnerable people under the means-tested minimum income scheme. Since the so-called refugee crisis, this has been especially crucial for the labour market integration of migrants, asylum seekers with subsidiary protection, and refugees – whose participation in the primary labour market has been limited by the increasing competition of low-skill and low-wage activities.

Another example of the City's institutional resilience to growing external pressures came shortly after the premature termination of the federal employment action plan, *Aktion 20,000*, which created 870 jobs in the secondary market for people over the age of 50 in Vienna in its first half-year. In response to its cancellation by the second conservative-right-wing federal government, the City of Vienna launched its own employment programme, *Joboffensive 50plus*, aimed at labour market reintegration for 500 people over the age of 50 who had been unemployed for more than three months. Vienna's steering capacity becomes clear through details: the programme covers the labour costs (up to 100%) for employment in community projects and social enterprises, and up to 66.7% for employment in private businesses. Additionally, as the City's main coordinator of the European Employment Strategy, WAFF has been able to formulate needs-oriented activation programmes for those who would have otherwise been excluded from public employment services. The financial capacity of WAFF has increased in recent years, not least due to the resources from the European Social Fund, which corresponded to almost one-third of its total expenditure in 2018 (18.1 million EUR).

Similarly, the City's new minimum income scheme diverged from the federal reform plan that was set to restrict access for large families and refugees to non-contributory social assistance. Vienna's regional social protection system has been crucial for the growing number of refugees (ca. 37% of all benefits recipients, as of 2019). This has been especially the case for asylum seekers with subsidiary protection, whose integration into the primary labour market, and therefore access to federal welfare programmes is limited. Unlike other *Bundesländer* that introduced the new federal social benefit scheme, as of 2021, Vienna has begun to provide asylum seekers with subsidiary protection with the residency-based benefit to the value of up to 949.46 EUR a month. This evidences the particular inclusiveness in Vienna's localised welfare system, as access to the minimum income scheme automatically qualifies the recipient for the contribution-based services provided by the AMS, which would otherwise only be available for those with employment records longer than six months in a year.

Conclusions

Since the early 1990s, emerging socioeconomic and political changes at multiple territorial levels have engendered both challenges and opportunities for Vienna's regulatory capacity and its ability to adequately address the increasing conditions of need. The shifting policy paradigm at the federal level has exacerbated the existing social inequalities in Vienna's urban labour market, in particular through increasingly restrictive conditionality for the social protection of marginalised, vulnerable groups outside of the labour force. Whilst the trend towards retrenchment and restrictions in social policies is a phenomenon that is not unique to Vienna or Austria, the regulatory framework at both levels have mediated the growing external pressures, which have in turn mitigated against the detrimental reform of its corporatist welfare system. At the City level, this owes much to the strong redistributive policy framework, of which the capacity for institutions to formulate their own employment and social policies have made it possible to expand the boundaries of social inclusion beyond those of the federal welfare state. Furthermore, a high level of coordination between different public institutions based on a consensus-building model contributes to the relative policy stability at the local level. This has been especially true for Vienna, where strong coordination between the regional branch of the federal employment service (AMS) and the City's own employment fund (WAFF) reversed their institutional deficiencies and complemented the policy capacity of one another. This resilience and capacity for innovation in the policy system has led to localised outcomes in the transition from welfare to workfare. This has not only slowed down the pace of abrupt policy changes, but has also allowed resistance against the fundamental restructuring of its institutional environment towards more exclusionary measures. Moreover, many of the reform proposals of the federal conservative-right-wing coalition were withdrawn by the end of 2019, when the new conservative-green coalition came to power.

The recent COVID-19 pandemic, however, has put the City to the test once again with the worst labour market crisis since the end of the Second World War. Thanks to the institutional capacity that characterises Vienna, with its strong corporatist welfare model, it is still able to mitigate external shocks through its localised regulatory framework, despite growing challenges. For instance, when Austria entered a lockdown in early March 2020, the City of Vienna launched its first Corona Aid Package on March 15th, complementing federal measures with a first emergency budget of 85 million Euro, including funds for small and medium-sized enterprises and for WAFF. Whilst one of the most crucial policy responses has been the expansion of the federal 'short-time work' employment scheme, Kurzarbeit,[5] the path-dependent effect of the City's local welfare system remained particularly relevant for the protection of socially vulnerable groups. This is particularly true for young people below the age of 25, who are the largest share of participants in the AMS apprenticeship positions and training courses. As the gap between the available training programmes and young job seekers grew, the city government launched specific training packages for the promotion of youth labour mobility and youth labour market integration. This age group, alongside other benefit recipients excluded from the federal unemployment insurance scheme, have been further assisted by employment programmes through the new means-tested minimum income scheme, which gives them access to 'one-stop-shop' services that are provided both by the municipal social welfare office and the AMS Vienna. From this point of view, Vienna's localised welfare system continues to retain its inclusive dimension, resulting in a just redistributive outcome for a broader range of its citizens. The strong regulatory mechanisms, both at the federal and City levels, have prevented the worst labour market outcomes in the midst of the pandemic. However, a prolonged crisis and growing unemployment may alter the situation in the long term, putting the City of Vienna under increasing financial and political pressures on the city's minimum income scheme.

Notes

1 Whilst the Parity Commission declined after Austria's accession to the EU in 1995 and was made defunct from 1998, the Advisory Council for Economic and Social Affairs remains, providing a platform for policy coordination between the four social partners.
2 The social partners previously had no formal decision-making competence in the AMV.
3 Whilst the duration of the job protection was reduced to 100 days, any job offered to the recipient was considered to be 'acceptable', as long as the wage covered at least the 80% of the calculation base of the previously received unemployment benefit, and the commute does not exceed 2 hours for full-time and 1.5 hours for part-time employment contracts. After 120 days of the benefit payment, this is reduced to 75%.
4 Since the Flexicurity Law Package in 2007, the legal criteria for the 'reasonableness' of labour market reintegration were extended to temporary employment in the secondary labour market via community projects and social enterprises.
5 It covers up to 90% of salaries for the amount of reduced work-hours in order to avoid mass layoffs. In March alone, the share of short-term working covered more than 58.6% of all activation programs, which subsidised 112,686 jobs.

References

Atzmüller, R., 2009. Institution building and active labour market policies in Vienna since the 1990s. *International Journal of Sociology and Social Policy*, 29(11/12), pp. 599–611.
Biffl, G., 1998. Placement activities in Austria before and after. *WIFO Working Papers*, 103, pp. 1–54.
Bonoli, G., 2010. The political economy of active labor-market policy. *Politics & Society*, 38(4), pp. 435–457.
Campbell, M., 2000. *Lokale Partnerschaften in Österreich: Eine Studie im Rahmen des LEED-Programmes der OECD*. Wien: Bundesministerium für Wirtschaft und Arbeit.

Deeg, R., 2007. Complementarity and institutional change in capitalist systems. *Journal of European Public Policy*, 14(4), pp. 611–630.
Gilbert, R.W., 1987. Austria's social partnership: A unique extralegal system of labor-management cooperation. *The Labor Lawyer*, 3(2), pp. 311–322.
Huber, P., 2004. Evaluating territorial employment pacts: Methodological and practical issues the experience of Austria. In: OECD, ed. 2004. *Evaluating local economic and employment development: How to assess what works among programmes and policies*. Paris: OECD Publishing, pp. 369–380.
Lechner, F., Reiter, W., Wetzel, P., et al., 2017. *Die experimentelle Arbeitsmarktpolitik der 1980er- und 1990er-Jahre in Österreich: Rückschlüsse und Perspektiven für Gegenwart und Zukunft der aktiven Arbeitsmarktpolitik*. Wien: Arbeitsmarktservice Österreich.
Leitner, A., Wroblewski, A., Hofer, H., et al., 2003. *Aktive Arbeitsmarktpolitik im Brennpunkt IX: Arbeitsmarktpolitische Wirkungen des TBP*. Wien: Arbeitsmarktservice Österreich.
Lewis, J., 2002. Austria in historical perspective: From civil war to social partnership. In: Berger, S. and Compston, H., eds., 2002. *Policy concertation and social partnership in Western Europe: Lessons for the 21st century*. New York: Berghahn Books, pp. 19–35.
Lutz, H. and Mahringer, H., 2007. Wirkt die Arbeitsmarktförderung in Österreich? Überblick über Ergebnisse einer Evaluierung der Instrumente der Arbeitsmarktförderung in Österreich. *WIFO Monatsberichte*, 3, pp. 199–218.
Natali, D., Pavolini, E. and Vanhercke, B., eds., 2018. *Occupational welfare in Europe: Risks, opportunities and social partner involvement*. Brussels: European Trade Union Institute (ETUI); European Social Observatory (OSE).
Obinger, H. and Tálos, E., 2006. *Sozialstaat Österreich zwischen Kontinuität und Umbau: Eine Bilanz der ÖVP/FPÖ/BZÖ-Koalition*. Vienna: VS Verlag für Sozialwissenschaften.
Österle, A. and Heitzmann, K., 2020. Austrification in welfare system change? An analysis of welfare system developments in Austria between 1998 and 2018. In: Blum, S., Kuhlmann, J. and Schubert, K., eds., 2020. *Routledge handbook of European welfare systems*. Abingdon, Oxon, New York: Routledge, pp. 21–37.
Tálos, E., 1987. Arbeitslosigkeit und beschäftigungspolitische Steuerung. In: E. Tálos and M. Wiederschwinger, eds. 1987. Arbeitslosigkeit: Österreichs Vollbeschäftigungspolitik am Ende? Vienna: Verlag für Gesellschaftskritik, pp. 91–166.
Tálos, E. and Hinterseer, T., 2019. *Sozialpartnerschaft: Ein zentraler politischer Gestaltungsfaktor der Zweiten Republik am Ende?* Innsbruck: Studienverlag.
Weishaupt, J.T., 2011. *Social partners and the governance of public employment services: Trends and experiences from Western Europe*. Geneva: International Labour Office.

7 Professionalisation, polarisation or both? Economic restructuring and new divisions of labour

Bernhard Riederer, Roland Verwiebe and Byeongsun Ahn

Introduction

Since the early 1990s, the Viennese economy has been characterised by large, public-owned industrial and service companies, focusing on the domestic Austrian market. Today, Vienna is one of the leading European cities of innovation, ranking among the top five of the first-tier metropolitan regions (Mayerhofer et al., 2015). Economic restructuring and internationalisation have left their mark on the Viennese labour market. The present chapter analyses the changes in the employment structure in the years since 1995 and the consequences for Vienna's social stratification, using both the labour force survey and administrative data. We hypothesise that tertiarisation and professionalisation have led to increasing polarisation among the Viennese working population. In addition, we argue that this process is strongly related to the immigration of both highly skilled professionals from other EU member states and low skilled labour from outside of Europe. Alongside these trends, women's participation in the labour market has increased, in particular with female part-time employment skyrocketing. Meanwhile, extended education and delayed retirement have altered the age composition of the working population. As a consequence, new social inequalities have emerged, whilst longstanding inequalities within the labour market persist.

Theoretical background: polarisation, resilience and professionalisation

The labour market is among the most important social institutions of modern societies, primarily responsible for the distribution of status and economic resources. Participation in the labour market is crucial to ensuring social inclusion, whilst a sustainable income is a prerequisite

DOI: 10.4324/9781003133827-10

for a decent standard of living. As such, both of these factors relate to issues of recognitional and distributional justice in general (Dahl et al., 2004; Fainstein, 2010). Inequalities in the labour market matter, especially in relation to justice. Individual problems 'cumulate into a pattern that can be traced to a systematic cause' which are 'rooted in structural features of society' (Nancy Fraser in Dahl et al., 2004, p. 378). In many cities across the globe, political leaders have increasingly bought into the 'competitiveness argument' (Fainstein, 2010). Though this approach might promote growth, it also aggravates existing maldistribution of economic recourses among vulnerable social groups. Tertiarisation and globalisation have led to a flexibilisation of the labour market, which has in turn contributed to the rise of new 'atypical' forms of employment, contributing to increasing social inequalities. Such patterns have affected Vienna, albeit to a different degree compared to many other European cities, as will be shown in the empirical part of the discussion.

Various strands of research have explicitly thematised the potential consequences of labour market transformations in today's cities. Most prominent in this context is the 'polarisation thesis' (Friedmann, 1986). Authors following this line of reasoning argue that economic changes lead to a polarisation of occupational structures (and thus social stratification), as cities become competitive centres of international production (e.g. Moulaert et al., 2003; Goos et al., 2009). Sassen (2016, p. 98), for instance, observes 'a sharp rise in the demand for both high-level talent and masses of low-wage workers' in urban economies. Migrants are often needed to satisfy both demands (Tai, 2006; McDowell et al., 2009; Sanderson et al., 2015). The increase in employment among the top and bottom occupational groups, along with a shrinking of occupational groups in the middle, lead to polarisation, nourished by growing international immigration.

Other authors argue that different cities present distinct scenarios of labour market transformation (Cucca and Ranci, 2017). This perspective considers the variegated governing capacities across cities (Fainstein, 2010, 2015), stressing the role of regional labour market policies and educational programmes in mediating place-specific economic and social transformation. Whilst the polarisation thesis refers to converging labour market trends in globalising cities, often rooted in the Anglo-American context, many European cities have retained distinctive welfare features, mitigating the negative spillovers of market relations (cf. Musterd and Ostendorf, 2013). In this respect, Vienna has frequently been portrayed as representative of the 'European City' (Le Galès, 2002), characterised by high resilience. Like many other

European cities, however, Vienna has also experienced a deep economic transition with significant impacts on local labour markets.

Beside the issue of cities' resilience, some authors stress the relevance of professionalisation, even perceiving this as the dominant process (e.g. Hamnett, 2015). They argue that increased demand for higher qualifications and specific occupational skills have led to an 'ongoing trend towards social upgrading', a decline in the size of the traditional working class and, thus, middle-class expansion (Cunningham and Savage, 2017, p. 26). Indeed, the share of professionals and higher-income classes has expanded substantially over the past decades in many major cities (Hamnett, 2020) – including New York, London (Butler et al., 2008; Hamnett, 2015), Paris (Clerval, 2020), Johannesburg (Crankshaw, 2017), Tokyo (van Ham et al., 2020), Hong Kong, Singapore (Tai, 2006) and Vienna (Riederer et al., 2019).

Vienna's economic structure: long-term developments

Despite a continuous economic decline since the 1973 oil crisis, unemployment remained low until the mid-1980s, with large public-owned industrial and service companies dominating the Viennese economy. Declining employment in the industrial sector emerged, not only from the trend towards deindustrialisation, but also from a lack of internationalisation, technological improvement and specialisation of industries. Traditional manufacturing industries like textile or consumer electronics continued to decline, whereas chemical production and mechanical engineering have grown from the 1980s onwards (Mayerhofer and Palme, 1997).

The restructuring of manufacturing and traditional service industries engendered a steady decline in employment throughout the 1990s. At the turn of the century, however, quality improvements in economic activities and growing investment in the technology- and knowledge-intensive service industries brought about positive developments. Growth was particularly remarkable in professional, technical, administrative and support services, indicating increasing specialisation (Hamnett, 2020). Between 1997 and 2007, high-technology, knowledge-intensive activities and knowledge-intensive market service activities in the tertiary sector have seen a sharp increase in total revenue (Mayerhofer et al., 2015).

Employment and expenditure in research and development have steadily grown since the early 2000s, in particular in medium-high-tech manufacturing, such as electronic equipment or machinery equipment and high-tech, knowledge-intensive services, such as information- and bio-technology. Meanwhile, Vienna is among the top European capital regions in science and technology. In 2017, the City spent 3.6% of its total expenditure on research and development activities. Vienna is well situated among major European metropolitan regions in terms of employment in the high-technology sectors in the active labour market population (Vienna: 7.0%, Berlin: 7.5%, Hamburg: 5.6%, Madrid 7.9%; Eurostat 2021). Non-enterprise research activities are mostly found in the higher education sector, which employs nearly 70% of all researchers in the city. Specialisation is most visible in employment within computer programming, consultancy and related activities. In terms of investment, biotechnology is now dominating the city's research and development sector, which has also been ranked among the top European cities in terms of patent application (Mayerhofer et al., 2015). In the past two decades, unemployment has nevertheless been exacerbated by steady population growth, mainly driven by immigration.[1] Together with the economic crisis of 2008/2009 and the COVID-19 lockdowns in 2020, this engendered the marginalisation of specific social groups from labour market participation.

Employment and unemployment in Vienna 1995 to 2020

Since the mid-1990s, the Viennese labour market grew in absolute figures, both in terms of employment and unemployment, mainly due to immigration. The role of migration can be best demonstrated with the example of new EU member states. In 2008, 7,398 citizens of Bulgaria and Romania were employed in Vienna, compared to 28,937 in 2019 (BALI, 2021). In relative terms, the share of the working population among the Viennese aged 25–64 remained consistently between 1995 and 2019 at 72% (Statistics Austria, 2020; own calculation). This stability, however, hides deep change. Whilst the share of the labour force increased among the older population due to political efforts to reduce early retirement, it decreased among younger groups due to the growing size of the student population in the city and prolonged periods of education and training. Correspondingly, job growth was most pronounced in the education industry, but also substantial in information and communication services, as well as accommodation and food services. The following in-depth analyses are mainly based on Austrian Microcensus data (1995–2019), a compulsory labour force survey using a representative 1% sample of Austrian households (Statistics Austria, 2020). The analysis of unemployment exploits administrative data from 2008 to 2020 (BALI, 2021).

The process of tertiarisation accelerated in Vienna from 1995 to 2019 (Table 7.1). The share of manufacturing, construction and craft sector jobs among the employed Viennese population further declined throughout the period and at a much faster pace than average in Austria (1995/2019: 32 vs. 25%; Vienna 1995/2019: 25 vs. 15%). The shares of wholesale and retail trade or financial and insurance activities within the service sector decreased, whilst the shares of business related and personal activities, education or human health and social work activities increased. In parallel, the share of white-collar

Table 7.1 Employment in Vienna 1995–2019 (in %)

Vienna	1995	2000	2005	2010	2015	2019
Selected industries						
Manufacturing, construction, craft sector	25.1	21.1	18.6	15.9	14.2	15.0
Wholesale and retail trade, repair of motor vehicles	15.3	15.3	13.7	12.5	12.3	12.6
Finance, insurance	6.1	5.4	5.2	5.1	4.9	3.5
Business related, personal services	25.7	28.6	30.8	33.6	32.9	33.6
Education	5.2	6.8	6.5	7.4	8.8	8.9
Human health, social work	9.2	9.0	10.8	11.1	11.5	11.7
Type of employment						
White-collar workers	48.1	51.5	54.7	57.5	62.7	64.6
Civil servants	14.5	13.7	9.0	7.4	5.7	4.6
Blue-collar workers	27.2	24.8	22.3	20.3	18.8	18.6
Self-employment	8.9	9.1	13.6	14.6	12.6	12.2
Contributing family workers	1.3	0.9	0.4	0.1	0.2	0.1
Employment intensity (hours/week)						
Short part-time (≤20)	5.9	7.6	10.1	10.9	12.7	11.2
Long part-time (<36)	7.9	8.3	11.1	13.6	16.7	17.6
Full-time (36+)	86.1	84.1	78.8	75.6	70.6	71.2

Source: Austrian Microcensus 1995 to 2019 (Statistics Austria, 2020); employed respondents aged 25–64; own weighted calculation.
Notes: Industry-categorisation is based on NACE; *Business related and personal services* comprise (a) information and communication, (b) real estate activities, (c) professional, scientific and technical activities, (d) administrative and support service activities, (e) arts, entertainment and recreation, (f) transportation and storage and (g) other services. This heterogeneous category was necessary to compare changes in industries over time. *Self-employment* includes one-person businesses (6.6% in 2019), self-employed with employees (4.5%) and freelance employment contracts (1.0%).

workers grew and the share of blue-collar workers shrunk. Austerity measures and changes in public services law reduced the share of civil servants, as many positions were terminated after workers retired and new employees in the public sector became contract workers (without the privileged civil services status). Self-employment, on the contrary, gained in relevance and spread much faster in Vienna than in Austria in general.

Although Vienna shows the highest full-time share among employed women in Austria (Vienna: 57%, Austria: 46%), the *part-time revolution* also affected the country's capital. Shares of both short (≤20 hours/week) and long part-time employment (<36 hours/week) roughly doubled between 1995 and 2018 (Table 7.1). Part-time employment is much more common among women. In 1995, only 5% of men but 25% of women worked part-time; in 2019, this relates to 16% and 43%, respectively. The main reason for men working reduced hours is (further) education (29%), whereas women most frequently report care responsibilities (31%). In households with children under the age of 6, 89% of part-time women workers mention care reasons (Statistics Austria, 2020, own calculation with data for 2019). The spread of part-time work has created new inequalities on the labour market and beyond, particularly with regard to financial insecurity after divorce and low female pension claims (Riederer and Berghammer, 2020).

Illustrating an enduring high degree of resilience, other forms of atypical employment are of minor relevance to the Viennese labour market. Although marginal employment[2] gained in relevance, particularly in accommodation and food services, only 2% of all workers were marginally employed in 2018. Between 2005 and 2019, subcontracted labour increased from 2% to 3%, and temporary employment from 5% to 8% (and is thus only slightly higher than in Austria in general). The share of the temporary employment decreases with age (15% among 25- to 29-year-olds, 4% for 55- to 59-year-olds in 2019), indicating growing job insecurity among young career entrants (Statistics Austria, 2020, own calculation).

Unemployment in Vienna (10% in 2017) is still modest compared to cities like Naples (28%), Brussels (18%), Paris (13%) or Madrid (15%). It is, however, higher than in Austria in general (6%), other Austrian cities (Graz: 9%, Linz: 8%, Salzburg: 7%) and cities like Berlin (8%), Prague (7%) or London (5%; figures from Eurostat, 2021). Vienna's economic restructuring can also be characterised by increasing unemployment. In terms of the national definition used in the following (see Note below Figure 7.1), unemployment rose from 7% in 1995 (City of Vienna, 2020) to almost 12% in 2019 (Figure 7.1). At the same time,

Professionalisation, polarisation or both? 105

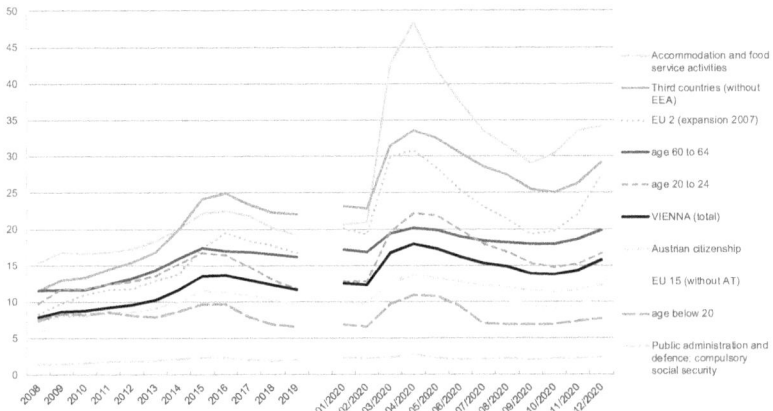

Figure 7.1 Development of the unemployment rate (national definition) in Vienna 2008–2020.

Source: BALI (2021), Authors' own illustration.

Note: The Austrian national definition of the unemployment rate expresses unemployment as a percentage of potential labour supply (sum of employed and unemployed) and does not include the self-employed.

differences in unemployment between various labour market groups started to increase. Unemployment barely changed in public administration (around 2%) or in the information and communication sector (slightly above 4%), whilst unemployment in accommodation and food service activities ascended to almost 23% in 2016. In particular, unemployment of non-EU migrants escalated to 25%, whereas unemployment of EU 15 migrants and Austrian citizens was much lower (10%–11%). Differences in unemployment also increased by age group, albeit to a lower degree.

The COVID-19 lockdowns in the spring and late autumn of 2020 significantly impacted on the Viennese labour market and accentuated existing social inequalities. In March and April, the unemployment rate (national definition) skyrocketed (Figure 7.1); in particular among (former) employees in accommodation and food services (48% in April). Given the seasonality of the tourism industry in Vienna, restaurants and hotels, which closed between mid-March and the end of May, suffered from less tourism during the summer. Unemployment also reached high levels (20% or more) in administrative and support services, construction, or arts, entertainment and recreation. Regarding nationality, already disadvantaged groups have been hit hardest.

Unemployment temporarily climbed above the 30% mark for non-EU migrants, as well as for Romanians and Bulgarians (EU 2). In contrast, citizens of the EU 15 countries experienced similar unemployment rates to Austrians at 13%. The age of workers also played a role: the largest increase in unemployment observed was for persons aged 20–24. Interestingly, the development of unemployment was very similar for both sexes. Vienna is an exception in this regard, because unemployment in other parts of Austria rose more steeply among women than men during the COVID-19 lockdowns (BALI, 2021). Presumably, women suffered more from the shutdown of the accommodation and food service industry, whereas men benefitted more from short-time work arrangements in manufacturing and booming construction work during the summer.

Changes in occupational class composition

The previous section showed that unemployment risks among societal subgroups have become increasingly unequal in Vienna. Here we focus on the distribution of the employed population across *occupational classes*, analysing our data with the widely used ISCO concept of the ILO, the *upper occupational class* comprises managers and professionals, the *upper middle-class* technicians and associate professionals, the *lower middle-class* clerical support workers, skilled agricultural, forestry and fishery workers, craft and related trades workers as well as plant and machine operators and assemblers, the *lower occupational class* service and sales workers as well as persons in elementary occupations. Descriptive results reveal *asymmetric polarisation tendencies*. The increase in the lower occupational classes between 1995 and 2019 was only modest, whilst the upper occupational classes grew from 26% to 36% (Figure 7.2).[3] The growth of the upper occupational classes was mainly due to the educational expansion (a rise in academic professions), whereas the share of managers decreased. Employment in lower class jobs grew due to a massive increase in routine service and sales jobs (from 11% to 18%). Unqualified manual jobs declined as deindustrialisation continued.

Changes in occupational class composition clearly differed by gender, age and nationality (Figure 7.2). First, professionalisation has been particularly strong among women, which might add a new quality to the urban professionalisation thesis (Hamnett, 2015; Sassen, 2016). Moreover, we can observe increasing polarisation for both sexes. Second, polarisation particularly concerns the younger age groups. Increases in both higher and lower occupational classes are observable among persons below 35. For those aged 35–49, the upper

Professionalisation, polarisation or both? 107

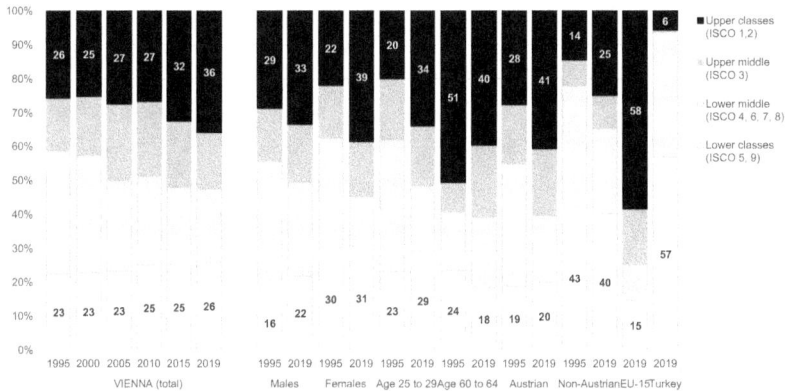

Figure 7.2 Changes in the distribution of occupational classes in Vienna 1995–2019.
Source: Austrian Microcensus 1995–2019 (Statistics Austria, 2020); employed respondents aged 25–64; own weighted calculation.
Note: Based on ISCO concept; the upper occupational classes comprise managers and professionals (ISCO 1, 2), the upper middle-class technicians and associate professionals (ISCO 3), the lower middle classes clerical support workers, skilled agricultural/forestry/fishery workers, craft and related trades workers, plant and machine operators/assemblers (ISCO 4, 6, 7, 8), the lower occupational classes service sales workers and elementary occupations (ISCO 5, 9).

class was growing, whereas, for persons aged 50–59, the rise in the lower class is larger than in the upper class. In the oldest age group (60–64), we even observe de-polarisation tendencies; presumably, because many of those who were not in managerial or professional positions were already retired at this age in 1995. Third, nationality matters. In 2019, a clear demarcation line exists between Austrians and EU 15 citizens (41% and 58% upper classes), on the one hand, and citizens of Eastern European EU countries (EU 12), successor states of former Yugoslavia, Turkey and other third countries (lower classes shares between 43% and 57%), on the other hand; indicating that heterogeneity of immigration could be a main driver of occupational polarisation (cf. McDowell et al., 2009; Riederer et al., 2019).

Next, we estimated multinomial logistic regression models to explain affiliation with lower, middle and upper occupational classes (Table 7.2). Results show that a position in manufacturing increases the probability of being a member of the middle classes, as it decreases the probability of belonging to upper or lower classes. Jobs in the trade sector are characterised by lower shares in the upper occupational classes and higher shares in lower occupational classes. In

Table 7.2 Determinants of occupational class in Vienna 1995 and 2019 (AME)

	1995		2019	
Occupational classes	Upper (ISCO 1, 2)	Lower (ISCO 5, 9)	Upper (ISCO 1, 2)	Lower (ISCO 5, 9)
	AME	AME	AME	AME
Industries				
Agriculture	-.36***	-.08	-.30***	-.23***
Manufacturing, construction, craft sector	-.19***	-.18***	-.09*	-.12***
Wholesale/retail trade, repair of motor vehicles	-.11***	.11***	-.11***	.15***
Accommodation, food services	-.18***	.48***	-.22***	.47***
Finance and insurance	-.19***	-.18***	.15***	-.22***
Business related, personal services	-.11***	-.02	.10***	-.07***
Public administration, social security	ref.	ref.	ref.	ref.
Education	.29***	-.18***	.39***	-.06**
Human health, social work	-.09***	.01	.19***	.03
Other services	-.03	-.13***	.02	-.03
Hours/week				
1–20	-.03	.11***	-.10***	.09***
21–35	.00	.08***	-.05***	.08***
36+	ref.	ref.	ref.	ref.
Gender				
Male	ref.	ref.	ref.	ref.
Female	-.10***	.09***	.00	.05***

Age in years				
25–34	−.03**	.00	.04***	−.02*
35–44	.00	.00	.08***	−.04***
45–54	ref.	ref.	ref.	ref.
55–64	.03	.01	.00	−.03*
Nationality				
Austria	ref.	ref.	ref.	ref.
EU 15 (without AT)			.16***	−.06***
EU 12			−.15***	.24***
Ex-Yugoslavia	−.21***	.37***	−.21***	.23***
Turkey	−.27***	.45***	−.33***	.39***
Other third countries			−.16***	
Other countries	.09***	−.03*		.16***

Source: Austrian Microcensus 1995 and 2019 (Statistics Austria, 2020); employed respondents aged 25–64; own weighted calculation.

Notes: For definitions, see notes below Figure 7.2 and Table 7.1. This table presents average marginal effects (AMEs) resulting from multinomial regression models. AMEs indicate higher or lower probabilities of belonging to an occupational class compared to a reference group (ref.; for example, public administration with regard to industries). The AME can also be understood as difference in the share of an occupational class compared to the reference group in terms of percentage points, where .02 means 2 p.p.; N_{1995} = 10,249; N_{2019} = 9,516; ***$p \leq .001$, **$p \leq .01$, *$p \leq .05$.

accommodation and food service activities, shares of middle and (particularly) lower class jobs are higher. In education, upper class jobs for professionals dominate. Educational expansion and an upgrading in vocational education and training also affected financial and insurance activities, business related and personal activities, health and social work. In 1995, the share of upper class jobs was lower in these industries than in public administration, but in 2019 the opposite was observable.

In line with the international literature (e.g. Halldén et al., 2012), analyses also reveal that part-time employment is more common than full-time employment in lower occupational class jobs. Additionally, in 2019, part-time work was less common in higher-class occupations (in particular short part-time, ≤20 hours/week). Part-time employment, however, was more common in lower middle-class manual positions. Regarding differences by gender, age groups or nationality, results of regression models confirm the descriptive results. As in many other countries and cities, the share of young people and women in upper class professions associated with higher skill levels increased (e.g. Black and Spitz-Oener, 2010). Meanwhile, the share of people in lower class jobs (middle-class positions) was still higher (lower) among women than men. Finally, non-EU 15-citizens, in particular from Turkey, were more likely to hold lower class positions compared to Austrians (in 1995 and 2019).

Additional decomposition analyses (not displayed in a table) show the impact of the changing composition of the labour force on occupational stratification in Vienna.[4] According to these analyses, about 3 percentage points of the 10-point increase in managerial and professional occupations and 4 percentage points of the 4-point increase in lower class jobs could be explained by the changing composition of the labour force between 1995 and 2019. In particular, the decrease in agricultural, manufacturing, construction and handicraft jobs contributed to both developments. Of similar relevance for the increase of managerial and professional occupations has been the growth of the educational sector. Meanwhile, an increase in jobs within accommodation and food service activities, as well as the increase in part-time employment and increasing immigration added most to the growth of lower class jobs.

Conclusions

Since the early 1980s, new demographic and economic trends began to reshape the labour market dynamics of European cities, pressuring the traditional balance between economic competitiveness and social cohesion (Cucca and Ranci, 2017). Drawing on the differentiated institutional and structural settings of cities, however, existing literature has shed light on the localised outcomes of equitable economic distribution, leading to different degrees of justice in the labour market (Fainstein, 2010). Indeed, the case of Vienna clearly demonstrates that urban social outcomes are affected by a specific set of factors, mainly by a decades-long tradition of state intervention and active labour market policies (see Ahn and Kazepov in this volume) and a massive influx of immigrants throughout the last 20 years.

With these two key factors in mind, the relatively high resilience of the Viennese labour market – reflected through a comparably low share of atypical forms of employment (except part-time arrangements) and, by international standards, quite modest levels of average unemployment – cannot be taken for granted. The rather strict regulatory framework and active labour market policies have often buffered negative consequences of economic developments and many flexibilisation trends set in much later in Vienna than in most other Western cities. Political measures (e.g. provisions of apprenticeship positions/training courses) may have also contributed to reducing youth unemployment in the aftermath of the economic crisis (2008/2009) to levels much lower than that of other cities. Although the local impact of deindustrialisation had been moderate in comparison to other traditional industrial cities in Europe, such as Manchester or Liverpool, substantial shifts in occupational classes have taken place over the last 25 years. Confirming results of previous studies on major cities (for an overview, see Hamnett, 2020), there has been a substantial growth in the class of professionals and managers. The development in Vienna may thus be best described as *asymmetrical polarisation*. Whilst professionalisation has been the dominating trend, a certain degree of polarisation (growing inequality) cannot be neglected.

Thus, new inequalities on the labour market have come into existence over recent years. Ambivalent developments concern women, youth and migrants. First, an increasing share of highly educated women hold professional and managerial positions, but at the same time, an increasing proportion of women are in part-time jobs and thus face higher risk of poverty after retirement or in the event of getting divorced (Halldén et al., 2012; Riederer and Berghammer, 2020). Second, the number of young people in professions associated with high skill levels increased, whilst younger age groups were also particularly affected by temporary employment and are therefore more vulnerable. Third, labour migrants from the 1960s and 1970s and other long-term migrants suffered from social decline, whereas more recent migrants improved their income positions due to higher levels of qualification (Riederer et al., 2019). As such, in line with many other major cities (Tai, 2006; McDowell et al., 2009), the main development in Vienna is the increasing polarisation within the migrant population. These days, Viennese residents from Turkey and other third countries are characterised by both higher shares of unemployment and lower class occupations, whereas citizens of EU 15 countries tend to be even more successful on the Viennese labour market than Austrian citizens. Finally, previously existing differences in unemployment are more pronounced after the COVID-19 lockdowns than any other period in Vienna throughout the last 25 years. Against the background of these findings, relating to the concept of the *just city*, our conclusion is obvious: the Viennese labour market has managed deindustrialisation quite well overall and is offering fairly paid jobs for a large majority of domestic workers. However, others are less well off in Vienna, especially the growing group of migrants from non-EU countries, who are often working under poor conditions and are facing much higher unemployment risks. This raises a substantial justice problem in our view that needs to be addressed by the citizens of the city, City officials, as well as employers in the immediate future.

Notes

1 Vienna has been more affected by migration than Austria, on average. In January 2020, 37% of the Viennese population were classified as foreign-born, compared to 20% of the Austrian population. About 13% of migrants in Vienna were born in the EU 15 member states, 23% in EU 12 countries, 25% in successor states of the former Yugoslavia (except Slovenia), 9% in Turkey and 30% in other countries. The largest migrant groups are Serbian (~90,000), Turkish, German, Rumanian, Bosnian and Syrian (~25,000) origin (Statistics Austria 2021; own calculation).
2 *Marginal employment* refers to low salaries (below EUR 446.81 per month in 2019). If this threshold is exceeded, mandatory contributions for health and pension insurance have to be paid in Austria.
3 Trends have been similar across Austria in general, albeit to different degrees. The share of upper occupational classes increased from 18% in 1995 to 27% in 2019, and the share of lower occupational classes from 22% to 25% (Statistics Austria, 2020, own calculation).
4 This analysis is based upon binary logistic regression models (Fairlie 2005).

References

BALI, 2021. *Beschäftigung: Arbeitsmarkt: LeistungsbezieherInnen: Informationen.* [online] Available at: https://bit.ly/2SRiTu1 [Accessed 17 May 2021].

Black, S. and Spitz-Oener, A., 2010. Explaining women's success: Technological change and the skill content of women's work. *Review of Economics and Statistics*, 92(1), pp. 187–194.

Butler, T., Hamnett, C. and Ramsden, M., 2008. Inward and upward: Marking out social class change in London, 1981–2001. *Urban Studies*, 45(1), pp. 67–88.

City of Vienna, 2020. *Arbeitslosenquoten in Wien nach nationaler und internationaler Definition nach Geschlecht seit 1995.* [online] Available at: https://bit.ly/3fnkiAm [Accessed 17 May 2021].

Clerval, A., 2020. Gentrification and social classes in Paris, 1982–2008. *Urban Geography* (online first). https://bit.ly/3eTbx1N

Crankshaw, O., 2017. Social polarization in global cities: Measuring changes in earnings and occupation inequality. *Regional Studies*, 51(11), pp. 1612–1621.

Cucca, R. and Ranci, C., 2017. *Unequal cities: The challenges of post-industrial transition in times of austerity.* London: Routledge.

Cunningham, N. and Savage, M., 2017. An intensifying and elite city: New geographies of social class and inequality in contemporary London. *City*, 21(1), pp. 25–46.

Dahl, M., Stoltz, P. and Willig, R., 2004. Recognition, redistribution and representation in capitalist global society. An interview with Nancy Fraser. *Acta Sociologica*, 47(4), pp. 374–382.

Eurostat, 2021. *Regions and cities illustrated.* [online] Available at: https://bit.ly/3eTeLCz [Accessed 17 May 2021].

Fainstein, S., 2010. *The just city.* Ithaca, NY: Cornell University Press.

Fainstein, S., 2015. Resilience and Justice. *International Journal of Urban and Regional Research*, 39(1), pp. 157–167.

Fairlie, R.W., 2005. An extension of the Blinder-Oaxaca decomposition technique to logit and probit models. *Journal of Economic and Social Measurement*, 30(4), pp. 305–316.

Friedmann, J., 1986. The world city hypothesis. *Development and Change*, 17(1), pp. 69–83.

Goos, M., Manning, A. and Salomons, A., 2009. Job polarization in Europe. *American Economic Review: Papers & Proceedings*, 99(2), pp. 58–63.

Halldén, K., Gallie, D. and Zhou, Y., 2012. The skills and autonomy of female part-time work in Britain and Sweden. *Research in Social Stratification and Mobility*, 30(2), pp. 187–201.

Hamnett, C., 2015. The changing occupational class composition of London. *City*, 19(2–3), pp. 239–246.

Hamnett, C., 2020. The changing social structure of global cities: Professionalization, proletarianisation or polarisation. *Urban Studies* (online first). doi:https://bit.ly/3hwIz9R

Le Galès, P., 2002. *European cities: Social conflicts and governance.* Oxford: Oxford University Press.

Mayerhofer, P., Firgo, M. and Schönfelder, S., 2015. 4. *Bericht zur internationalen Wettbewerbsfähigkeit Wiens.* [pdf] Available at: https://bit.ly/2RgSkyh [Accessed 17 May 2021].

Mayerhofer, P. and Palme, G., 1997. Deindustrialisierung in Wien: Phänomen der Stadtentwicklung oder Ausdruck von Wettbewerbsschwächen? *WIFO Monatsberichte*, 8, pp. 485–499.

McDowell, L., Batnitzky, A. and Dyer, S., 2009. Precarious work and economic migration: Emerging immigrant divisions of labour in Greater London's service sector. *International Journal of Urban and Regional Research*, 33(1), pp. 3–25.

Moulaert, F., Arantxa, R. and Swyngedouw, E., eds., 2003. *The globalized city: Economic restructuring and social polarization in European cities*. Oxford: Oxford University Press.

Musterd, S. and Ostendorf, W., eds., 2013. *Urban segregation and the welfare state: Inequality and exclusion in Western cities*. London: Routledge.

Riederer, B. and Berghammer, C., 2020. The part-time revolution: changes in the parenthood effect on women's employment in Austria across the birth cohorts from 1940 to 1979. *European Sociological Review*, 36(2), pp. 284–302.

Riederer, B., Verwiebe, R. and Seewann, L., 2019. On changing social stratification in Vienna: Why are migrants declining from the middle of society? *Population, Space and Place*, 25(2). doi:https://bit.ly/3ygcxVm

Sanderson, M.R., Derudder, B., Timberlake, M. and Witlox, F., 2015. Are world cities also world immigrant cities? An international, cross-city analysis of global centrality and immigration. *International Journal of Comparative Sociology*, 56(3–4), pp. 173–197.

Sassen, S., 2016. The global city: Enabling economic intermediation and bearing its costs. *City & Community*, 15(2), pp. 97–108.

Statistics Austria, 2020. *Mikrozensus*. [online] Available at: https://bit.ly/2SYS3QT [Accessed 17 May 2021].

Statistics Austria, 2021. *Bevölkerung nach Staatsangehörigkeit und Geburtsland*. [online] Available at: https://bit.ly/3yaRB1Y [Accessed 17 May 2021].

Tai, P.-F., 2006. Social polarisation: Comparing Singapore, Hong Kong and Taipei. *Urban Studies*, 43(10), pp. 1737–1756.

van Ham, M., Uesugi, M., Tammaru, T., Manley, D. and Janssen, H., 2020. Changing occupational structures and residential segregation in New York, London and Tokyo. *Nature Human Behaviour*, 4, pp. 1124–1134.

Part IV
Environment

8 Vienna's urban green space planning
Great stability amid global change

Anna-Katharina Brenner, Elisabetta Mocca, and Michael Friesenecker

Introduction

Urban green space (hereafter UGS) planning has been concerned with how to introduce and institutionalise new governing policies that encourage specific qualities of green spaces, considering both social and environmental dimensions. UGS is a comprehensive term, indicating areas of vegetation in an urban landscape, and has been associated with several benefits in terms of residents' health and wellbeing (e.g. Maas et al., 2006). Historically, UGS has been employed as a planning tool to approach various social problems, whilst its value in adapting to the negative impacts of the climate crisis has only recently gained importance (Loughran, 2020).

From a theoretical standpoint, environmental justice (EJ) research emphasises how these positive effects (as well as environmental hazards) associated with UGS are often spatially unequally distributed in cities (Walker, 2012). Whilst a growing number of studies on European cities have analysed the (uneven) distribution and availability of UGS per inhabitant (see Kabisch et al., 2016), too little is known about how urban conditions and their transformation over time have put pressure on the availability of UGS to diverse social groups (Rutt and Gulsrud, 2016). From a political perspective, it has been noted that social-democratic welfare states appear to better integrate social and environmental policies than liberal market economies (Dryzek, 2003), as they make 'conscious and coordinated' efforts to mutually reinforce ecologic and economic values (Gough et al., 2008, pp. 334–335). Yet, according to Rutt and Gulsrud (2016, p. 124), 'if and how urban managers take up issues of diversity and inclusion in their daily and strategic UGS management' remains an under-researched topic.

DOI: 10.4324/9781003133827-12

118 *Anna-Katharina Brenner et al.*

Against this background, Vienna constitutes an interesting case study, as it has maintained its high share of UGS (almost 50% of the city area) over the past 30 years. Compared to other European cities, Vienna has been a pioneer in UGS planning (Anguelovski et al., 2018). However, over the last three decades, the city has experienced a set of profound transformations, including population growth, sociodemographic shifts, increasing inequalities (Riederer et al., 2019), environmental changes (in particular shifting weather events), and new governing arrangements as a result of Austria's accession to the European Union. Therefore, we aim to investigate how these transformations have shaped Vienna's UGS policies, its institutional settings, and formal and informal rules (Sorensen, 2017), as well as their outcomes in terms of just provision of UGS.

EJ, operationalised through the concepts of distribution and recognition, will be adopted to analyse two key policy dimensions. First, we were interested in the institutional setting and ideals/values of Vienna's strategic UGS policy and how it has changed over time. In particular, this chapter will examine how population growth and changing multi-level arrangements in the last 30 years have modified UGS-related planning in Vienna. That aim implies a focus on how different needs have come to be recognised in strategic planning documents. We performed an extensive literature review and document analysis concerning UGS in Vienna, covering the 30-year reference period to investigate the evolution of Vienna's UGS policy. Expert interviews supplemented the document analysis. Second, we examine how UGS policy has shaped the distribution and availability of green spaces. In so doing, we used availability as a simple indicator (Kronenberg et al., 2020) to analyse whether residents have access to UGS in close proximity to where they live. The amount of UGS per inhabitant within a 250 m radius was in focus, and we analyse changes in availability between 2001 and 2018.

Vienna's UGS governance: a complex set of public actors

The institutional setting of UGS governance in Vienna is shaped by a complex network of public actors across different governing levels. At the municipal level, three main actors shape UGS governance: The Municipal Department of Urban Planning (MA18), the Municipal Department for Environmental Protection (MA22), and the Municipal Department for District Planning and Land Use (MA21). The former is responsible for devising strategic, non-binding urban development plans (*Stadtentwicklungsplan*, hereafter STEP), including (spatial) UGS concepts after being approved by the city council, which shape ideals and values. The MA22, established during the 1980s, is responsible for the implementation of regional, federal and the EU legal frameworks in the field of nature protection. The MA21, in charge of the land zoning process, implements the strategic non-binding urban development plans, including the zoning of nature protected areas, which is regulated by the Viennese Building Code (BO). Thus, the latter is an important instrument in shaping the distribution of UGS across the city. Other relevant municipal departments responsible for administrating UGS are the Municipal Department for Parks and Gardens (MA42) and the Municipal Department of the Forestry Office and Urban Agriculture (MA49). The budget for the Planning Department is limited. But the latter two bodies account for a considerable proportion of the City expenditures. Between 1999 and 2019, they spent 1% of the City's budget annually, whilst the absolute expenditures increased to about 100 million Euros per annum (MA5, 2020).

Changes in the City Statute in 1988 endowed the 23 districts of Vienna with greater responsibilities, whilst the budget was transferred on a task-specific basis. Within this decentralised system, districts are responsible for planning, constructing, renewing and maintaining UGS in cooperation with responsible municipal departments. Investments in UGS differ quite substantially between the districts (from 5% to 18% in 2019), depending on the districts' amount of green space that needs to be maintained as well as activities to extend UGS. However, these 'local' budgets mainly cover maintenance, leaving only a small portion to expand UGS. Thus, districts normally apply for additional financial resources from central city resources for such activities.

UGS managed by the districts mainly include small-scale greening initiatives, whereas large-scale green areas (such as some parks and cemeteries) fall under the responsibility of the City. Furthermore, influence from the federal level on Vienna's UGS governance is limited to the design and maintenance of seven federal gardens (such as the famous '*Schönbrunn Gardens*'). A legacy of the *Habsburg Era*, these gardens contribute to shaping the image of the city and constitute important tourism attractions. Nevertheless, the federal level has little to no influence on UGS planning, in contrast to the increasing influence of the EU, which will be discussed in more detail in the next section.

Vienna's changing UGS policy: between urban development and urban renewal

In policy discourses, UGS is historically tied to (industrial) urbanisation and population growth. Hence, some European cities have focused on the maintenance and legal protection of their green belts to attenuate urban sprawl, to provide urban dwellers with access to forestry, agriculture, and recreational areas, and to secure ecological functions, such as the provision of fresh air (Bishop et al., 2020). The history of modern UGS planning spans over a century in Vienna, and its development has been shaped by a range of institutional actors across multiple governing levels, as illustrated in Figure 8.1. In 1905, given the rapid expansion of the urban boundaries, the council decided to legally protect the Viennese forest and meadow belt, mostly covering the western outskirts of the city (Breiling and Ruland, 2008, p. 170) to ensure the provision of clean air to citizens and protect Vienna's wilderness. Although initiated in a period characterised by *Municipal Populism* under Mayor Karl Lueger (Suitner, 2020, p. 10), the institutionalisation of the protection of the green belt represents a first milestone in the city's history. The social and health-oriented UGS approach of the city government was crucially shaped by the protection of the Viennese green belt, during the Red Vienna period, after the Second World War, and has an impact even today.

Between the 1960s and 1980s, when many residents moved from the dense inner-city districts to housing estates in the peripheral districts, the Social-Democratic City Government implemented large-scale projects at the periphery (Rode and Schwab, 2017). Probably the most iconic project of this era is the Danube Island (*Donauinsel*). On the one hand, this work sought to control flooding; on the other hand, it provided the city with wide green recreational areas.

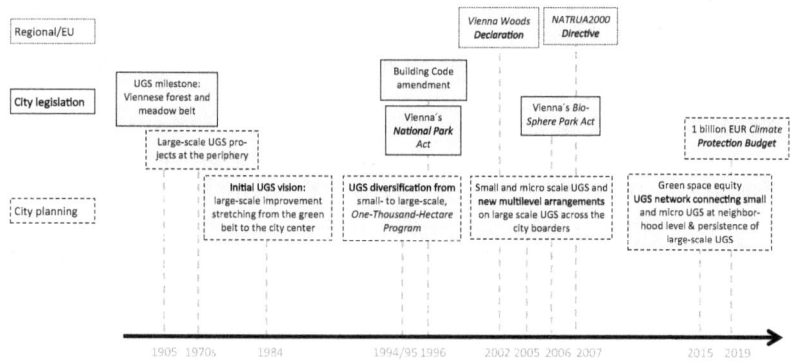

Figure 8.1 Timeline of central UGS policies at different governing levels between 1905 and 2019.

Source: Authors' own.

Recent developments in large-scale UGS protection

Vienna's first urban development plan, approved by the city council in 1984, emphasised the necessity of improving the population's living conditions through welfare-oriented economic development and by protecting, maintaining and developing healthy and liveable environments to counter the city's population decline, driven by suburbanisation (MA18, 1984, p. 11). To this end, the plan proposed a shift from the dominant focus on the urban development of previous decades towards urban renewal, de-densification and expansion of UGS in densely populated inner-city areas. Children, young people, and the elderly were considered to be particularly exposed by the existing urban conditions; thus, UGS was to be designed considering their needs. Nevertheless, the strategic planning vision focused on large-scale improvements, such as green corridors, green patches, and green islands to connect inner-city areas with the parts of the green belt (MA18, 1984, p. 76). This strategy makes Vienna a pioneering city in green space planning in the European context. Other cities, such as Stuttgart, Sheffield or Birmingham, adopted similar strategies in the 1990s, and in some cases (e.g. Leeds, Barcelona), even in the 2000s (Anguelovski et al., 2018).

Throughout the early 1990s, UGS policy had to come to terms with population growth. Furthermore, as a result of Austria's accession to the EU in 1995, the city council expected Vienna to be exposed to competitive conditions within the single market. Yet, EU membership was seen as a chance to establish Vienna as a regional economic centre (Mocca et al., 2020). In effect, throughout the 1990s, the dominant narrative was characterised by a positive attitude towards moderate urban expansion and growth. That attitude framed the protection, maintenance, and expansion of UGS vis-á-vis pressures from urban development and new housing construction. Similar to other UGS leading cities of today, such as Copenhagen, the management of UGS in urban development areas acquired greater importance for the administration in this period (Anguelovski et al., 2018). The 1994 plan defined quantitative criteria that should guarantee 3–5 m^2 of UGS per inhabitant as a non-binding guideline. Nevertheless, the administration refrained from applying these criteria to inner-city areas because of the structural preconditions but a commitment to small-scale improvements was set up (MA18, 1994). Recognising the different needs of certain social groups in the UGS planning process, women's needs, especially working mothers, were accounted for as part of the gender mainstreaming trend sweeping through Vienna's agencies.

Against the changing demographic and economic context mentioned above, the city government primarily sought to secure its large-scale UGS. Most importantly, the council passed a resolution, the so-called *One-Thousand-Hectare Program*, to expand the green belt in 1995. This resolution mainly aimed at the legal protection of the existing green belt through new zoning schemes and extending the belt in the previously unprotected north-eastern parts of Vienna by buying urban land. In achieving the former, the building code was amended in 1996, and a new legal act – the so-called *Vienna's National Park Act* – was implemented to adapt the legal framework of nature protection. Changes to the building code comprised new zoning categories that specifically designated legally protected areas in the green belt, including agricultural land and selected parks. These zoning categories are Vienna's highest UGS protection measures, as they are equivalent to a building ban, and it is hard to rezone these areas for other purposes. At that time, not many other European cities strived for such a large-scale and sustainable preservation of UGS. Those who did, such as Marseille, had similar financing problems in the face of population growth (Anguelovski et al., 2018). By 2003, 95% of the planned areas were put under these kinds of zoning categories, whereby only a small share of UGS located in the green belt was bought by the City (Rechnungshof Österreich, 2005). Population growth was under-estimated by the council and increasing housing demand led to a worrying scarcity of building land and soaring land prices – factors that made the acquisition of UGS by the city difficult (Rechnungshof Österreich, 2005).

The impact of changing multi-level arrangements

Influenced by the EU's 'calls for sustainable, yet competitive territorial development', urban planning shifted in the early 2000s towards a 'managerial' governance style, characterised by the involvement of non-public actors (Suitner, 2020, p. 15). Additionally, regional economic policy became as important as the social and environmental policies of the previous decades, which aimed at ensuring equal opportunities and an adequate quality of life for all residents. The following quote from the 2005 Urban Development Plan (*STEP05*, see Figure 8.1) exemplifies this shift in urban development – which can also be observed in other European UGS pioneer cities such as Copenhagen and Munich (Anguelovski et al., 2018):

> In a development geared towards sustainability, the maintenance and further development of the landscapes and the green and

open spaces represent an integral component of economic locational development and is a basis of the long-term preservation of the quality of life.

(MA18, 2005, p. 55)

Given the growth of an increasingly demographically diversified population resulting from migration to Vienna following the Fall of the Iron Curtain (1989), the Yugoslav Wars (1991–2001), and the eastward enlargement of the EU (2004), UGS planning sought to acknowledge different needs, signalling an increasingly spatially differentiated approach to UGS development. Simultaneously, the 'steep population growth' prompted the administration to recognise the uneven distribution of green spaces (MA18, 2005, p. 19). The plan acknowledged that low-income neighbourhoods were characterised by inadequate housing conditions and a lack of large green spaces. That led to a change in the City's spatial vision: in addition to large-scale development, small and micro-scale approaches began to be seen as crucial to meet the needs of different ethnic groups and urban dwellers with disabilities. This vision foresaw the expansion and renewal of existing green spaces and further development of green spaces on inner-city brownfield sites. Moreover, the plan also introduced micro-scale greening of public spaces, such as squares, streets and pedestrian zones.

Although small-scale and micro-scale UGS are gaining importance in strategic planning, the new multi-level arrangement via Austria's accession to the EU increased the protection of large UGS across the city boundaries. New regulations such as the NATURA2000 Directive (the *Vienna Woods Declaration*) further secured and protected additional parts of the Vienna Woods including a UNESCO biosphere park in 2006 (Vienna's *Biosphere Park Act*) and the spring water protection forests in Lower Austria and Styria. These UGS provide the city with important ecological functions, such as high-quality water supply, fresh air and recreational areas for urban dwellers.

Towards small- and micro-scale improvements

Whilst the 2005 urban development plan marked a shift towards revitalising UGS development in densely built-up areas, the SPÖ-Greens coalition government formed in 2010 further intensified this shift. The uneven distribution of UGS was problematic for the administration, which had to deal with the effects of steep population growth, demographic challenges, and the impact of climate change. The city council began to recognise that the provision of large-scale UGS alone was insufficient to address urban environmental problems stemming from climate change, such as hotter and drier temperatures recognisable by the soaring increase in heat days (ZAMG-Klimaabteilung, 2019). In particular, elderly and deprived urban dwellers living in dense, inner-city areas affected by urban heat island effects have been increasingly recognised as vulnerable groups by the administration.

Inspired by UGS planning strategies of other European cities, such as Stockholm and Amsterdam, in 2015 the city council approved Vienna's Thematic Concept for Green and Open Spaces, which integrates – for the first time in Vienna's history – the general principle of *Green Space Equity*. As an urban planning principle, green space equity implies that 'all citizens have the same right to the high-quality provision of green and open space' (MA18, 2015, p. 15). Green space equity is operationalised as the availability of 3.5 m^2 of UGS per inhabitant within a distance of 250 m for all urban dwellers (MA18, 2015, p. 84). That includes the creation of lively and green streetscapes and pedestrian zones (e.g. *Mariahilferstraße* or *Kärntnerstraße*), of green elements in the streets, including adjacent green spaces (e.g. *Ringstraße, Grätzl Oase*), of façade greenery and the greening of brownfields (e.g. *Gaudenzdorfer Gürtel*).

The concept marked a clear discursive shift towards improving green spaces at the immediate neighbourhood scale and pre-structures the application of different green space types according to urban forms and changing needs of urban dwellers. Here, the expected demographic changes, where the proportion of elderly and migrant populations were predicted to increase, led to shifts in requirements for the design and quality of UGS. Access to larger UGS recreational areas should be granted for all urban dwellers by public transport. Thereby, the traditional city government's focus on securing large-scale UGS and prioritising the provision of parks and vast recreational areas at the city fringes persisted. The new aspect in this was the development of a *Green Space Network Plan*, creating and connecting distributed micro- and small-scale UGS. That included greening measures targeting streets and pedestrian zones, reclaiming public space from motorised-individual transport. Thus, opening a new discussion concerning the fair distribution of public space linked to the increasingly noticeable effects of climate change.

The implementation of small and micro-spaces, however, has proved to be difficult in the current multi-level setting. For example, districts have the authority to enforce or delay greening strategies as a result of the additional UGS planning competencies they were granted in 1998. The reclamation of parking spaces to make room for urban green remains conflictual due to opposing interests of residents, district representatives, urban planners and administration, city politicians and social partners. However, this conflictual dynamic is slowly changing in light of hotter and drier temperatures. By enforcing local small-scale greening measures, urban dwellers and district representatives are starting to cooperate, also in districts that are relatively car-dominated.

Additionally, as district budgets mainly cater for the maintenance of existing UGS, substantial challenges have arisen in the funding of additional UGS. The cost of planting a tree, for instance, can be high, varying between 300 and 3,000 Euros – costing more in less favourable conditions, such as densely built urban areas. Therefore, districts need a high commitment to UGS implementation and depend on additional financial aid. In this respect, it is important to note the 1-billion Euro climate protection budget approved by the city government in 2019, of which 64 million Euros were devoted to expanding and improving parks and green spaces, and a 2.3 million Euro funding package for cooling efforts to adapt to urban heat islands on a local scale (Oeko-BusinessWien, 2019). An additional source of funding for districts is EU-funded local development programs, by which some local UGS projects have been implemented (see City of Vienna, 2013).

The availability of UGS

We now turn to the analysis of how the availability of UGS per inhabitant at the neighbourhood level changed in the period under consideration (see Figure 8.2). In Vienna, the shares of UGS in densely built and populated inner-city districts range from 2% to 15% (from the city centre within the Ring to areas between the Ring and the Gürtel). In the fringe districts, UGS shares range from 40% to 70%. Our analysis of UGS availability builds on the supply standards defined by the City for Green Space Equity. We applied the 3.5 m^2 UGS per inhabitant within 250m threshold as the availability of UGS proxy.[1] The spatial analysis shows most of the statistical units are well-served with an adequate amount of green space. A recent study conducted by the City of Vienna found that two-thirds of Vienna's dwellers live a maximum of 250m from the closest publicly accessible UGS (MA22, 2015). Our analysis found that in 2018 about 92% of the population are adequately served with UGS. Differences might be explained by distinct statistical methods in the aggregation of UGS to the statistical units.

Nevertheless, persistent pockets exist within the city centre and between the Ring and Gürtel that have an inadequate supply of UGS

126 *Anna-Katharina Brenner et al.*

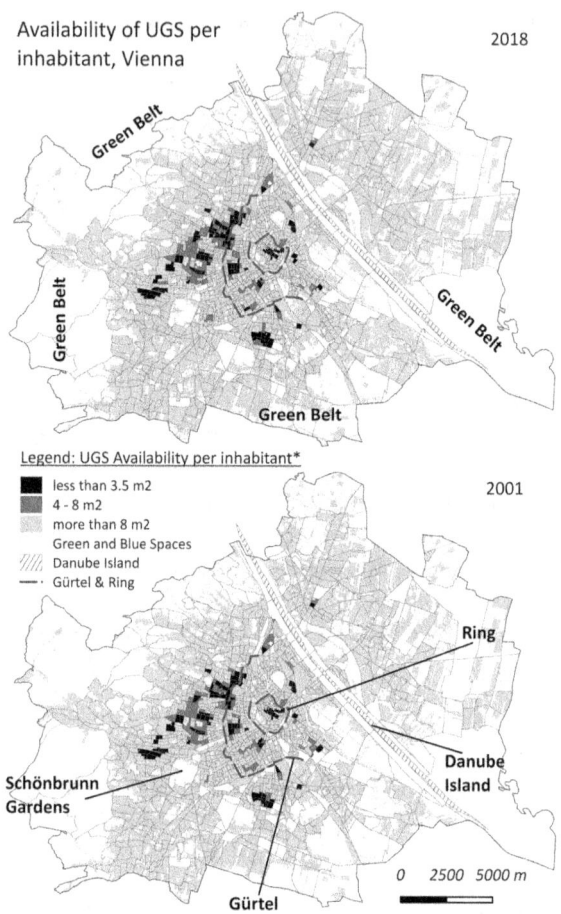

Figure 8.2 Availability of UGS per inhabitant, 2001 and 2018.
Sources: Land-Use Data: Stadt Wien – data.wien.gv.at, 2001 and 2018; Population Data: MA23 – Wirtschaft, Arbeit und Statistik.

(less than 3.5 m^2 per inhabitant). Most remarkable, however, is a larger agglomeration of statistical units lacking adequate UGS availability outside of the western Gürtel. These areas are partly marked by high shares of sub-standard apartments and a relative over-representation of low-skilled residents (Hatz et al., 2015). In contrast, the protected areas of the green belt mainly serve wealthier households in the surrounding western districts, especially in the 13th, 18th and 19th districts – characterised by the highest average net income in the city (Statistik Austria, 2019).

Although disparities exist, our analysis suggests that access to UGS is relatively widespread among the population, especially when considering the steep population growth of recent decades in Vienna. Between 2001 and 2018, the population increased by nearly 340,000, and the population density rose from 236 to 260 inhabitants per ha built-up area. In contrast, areas with less than 3.5 m^2 UGS per inhabitant declined by only 1%. That suggests that the City managed the population growth fairly well, which is related to the City's socially inclusive and environmentally friendly urban expansion (see Chapter 4 by Litschauer and Friesenecker in this volume). However, pressures on areas with scarce green spaces intensified, as displayed in Figure 8.2, since population density increased in already densely populated inner-city districts. Rising pressures might also be produced by different patterns of use of green spaces. In this regard, Höglhammer et al. (2019) show that immigrants from non-western countries are underrepresented in their use of the city's Biosphere Park in the green belt since they are not aware of its existence.

Conclusions

In this chapter, we analysed UGS development over the past 30 years. We employed EJ as an analytical concept that allowed us to identify how distribution and recognition in strategic planning have been addressed, encouraging different forms and qualities of places.

Since the beginning of the 20th century, the city government has promoted a socially and health-oriented UGS provision that fosters equal opportunities for everyone. Whilst other European cities have experienced a gradual shift towards more market-oriented management of UGS, especially in Central and Eastern Europe (Kronenberg et al., 2020), our analysis shows that Vienna's UGS governance was and continues to be characterised by a strong state-based approach. The city maintained its socially and health-oriented policy approach, and it provided more diverse types of UGS to adapt planning ideals/values to the different and changing needs of the population. Whether the groups targeted by such planning are actually attracted by the quality and design of UGS is not clear and requires further research. The introduction of the principle of *Green Space Equity* represents a change, emphasising the needs of UGS provision in the vicinity of residential locations. Compared to other 'green' cities, this egalitarian approach to UGS provision is rather a novelty. Amsterdam, for instance, has aimed to ensure access to UGS for all residents by a maximum of ten minutes' walk since 1935 (Anguelovski et al., 2018). Further, Austria's accession to the EU provided new regulations to protect UGS.

That strengthened the policy approach of the city government, which enhanced the protection of large parts of the green belt for present and future generations, thus making sustainability a crucial principle in UGS planning and management.

Considering UGS distribution, our findings showed that Vienna strived to widen the diffusion of UGS across the city. Whilst the UGS share has remained relatively stable over the last 30-year period, uneven patterns of available UGS m^2 per inhabitant have also remained stable. According to our results, although the majority are provided with a decent amount of green space, persistent pockets of underprovision exist. The aim to connect the city via green corridors shifted over time towards a more diverse distribution of green spaces throughout the city. Achievements were constantly challenged by increasing population density, path-dependent urbanisation patterns, and barriers to greening rooted in the institutional setting in inner-city areas. Of course, our measurements of UGS availability are a rough approximation of reality, thus not enabling us to draw any conclusions about the quality of UGS. Furthermore, we need to consider that problems related to the lack of green spaces might be compensated by Vienna's efficient public transport system, which brings residents in a relatively short time to larger green spaces. Finally, effects of climate mitigation might be contained by already existing small-scale UGS, not captured by the land-use data applied in this study.

However, to address necessary climate adaptation strategies and improve quality of life for all people in urban areas, further revitalising of UGS in densely populated urban areas is paramount. To date, the provision of large-scale UGS alone has proved to be insufficient. It remains to be seen whether the advancement of UGS is evolving fast enough, especially in densely built areas, to compensate for negative health impacts due to rising temperatures (especially for the elderly and deprived).

Note

1 In a GIS program, we calculated a 250 m catchment radius around land-use-based UGS zoning categories (cemeteries, parks, forests, meadows, vineyards, agrarian fields). Then we apportioned the data to the smallest available spatial unit (ca. 1,360 census tract). We merged the census tracts with information about the UGS share with the census tracts containing information about the total population. Some census tracts are only partly covered by the 250 m UGS catchment radius. Thus, we normalised the share of UGS by the ratio of the area of the catchment vis-á-vis the area of the census tracts. Finally, we divided the normalised share of UGS by the total population for each census tract.

References

Anguelovski, I., Argüelles, L., Baró Porras, F., Cole, H.; J. J.T., García-Lamarca, M., 2018. *Green Trajectories—Municipal policy trends and strategies for greening in Europe, Canada and United States (1990–2016).* [pdf] Available at: https://bit.ly/3cEPo6k [Accessed 01 April 2021].

Bishop, P., Martinez Perez, A., Roggema, R. and Williams, L., eds., 2020. *Repurposing the green belt in the 21st century.* UCL Press. https://bit.ly/3wlp2hv

Breiling, M. and Ruland, G., 2008. The Vienna green belt: From localised protection to a regional concept. In: Amati, M., ed., 2008. *Urban green belts in the twenty-first century.* London and New York: Routledge, pp. 167–183.

City of Vienna, 2013. *EU-Projekte für Wien-Überblick Förderprogramm-Regionale Wettbewerbsfähigkeit und integrative Stadtentwicklung.* [pdf] Available at: https://bit.ly/3u85lYC [Accessed 02 April 2021].

Dryzek, J.S., ed., 2003. *Green states and social movements: Environmentalism in the United States, United Kingdom, Germany, and Norway.* Oxford: Oxford University Press.

Gough, I., Meadowcroft, J., Dryzek, J., Gerhards, J., Lengfeld, H., Markandya, A. and Ortiz, R., 2008. JESP symposium: Climate change and social policy. *Journal of European Social Policy,* 18(4), pp. 325–344.

Hatz, G., Kohlbacher, J. and Reeger, U., 2015. Socio-economic segregation in Vienna: A social-oriented approach to urban planning and housing. In: Tammaru, T., Marcinczak, S., van Ham, M. and Musterd, S., eds., 2015. *Socio-economic segregation in European capital cities: East meets west.* London: Routledge, pp. 80–109.

Höglhammer, A., Muhar, A. and Stokowski, P., 2019. Access to and use of the Wienerwald Biosphere Reserve by Turkish and Chinese people living in Austria – Implications for planning. *Journal on Protected Mountain Areas Research,* 11(2), pp. 11–17.

Kabisch, N., Strohbach, M., Haase, D. and Kronenberg, J., 2016. Urban green space availability in European cities. *Ecological Indicators,* 70, pp. 586–596.

Kronenberg, J., Haase, A., Łaszkiewicz, E., Antal, A. Baravikova, A., Biernacka, M., Dushkova, D. et al., 2020. Environmental justice in the context of urban green space availability, accessibility, and attractiveness in post-socialist cities. *Cities,* 106, p. 102862.

Loughran, K., 2020. Urban parks and urban problems: An historical perspective on green space development as a cultural fix. *Urban Studies,* 57(11), pp. 2321–2338.

MA5, 2020. *Rechnungsabschluss—Budget der Stadt Wien.* [online] Available at: https://bit.ly/3rJDpIX [Accessed 02 April 2021]

MA18, 1984. *Stadtentwicklungsplan 1984.* [online] Available at: https://bit.ly/39BIVai [Accessed 02 April 2021].

MA18, 1994. *Stadtentwicklungsplan 1994.* [online] Available at: https://bit.ly/31GOq3a [Accessed 02 April 2021].

MA18, 2005. *Stadtentwicklungsplan 2005. Short Report.* [pdf] Available at: https://bit.ly/3rEk5wE [Accessed 02 April 2021].

MA18, 2015. *Thematic concept-green and open space.* [pdf] Available at: https://bit.ly/31TySt7 [Accessed 02 April 2021].

MA22, 2015. *Öffentlich zugängliche Grünflächen-Analyse.* [online] Available at: https://bit.ly/3cHO6HC [Accessed 02 April 2021].

Maas, J., Verheij, R.A., Groenewegen, P.P., De Vries, S. and Spreeuwenberg, P., 2006. Green space, urbanity, and health: How strong is the relation? *Journal of Epidemiology & Community Health,* 60(7), pp. 587–592.

Mocca, E., Friesenecker, M. and Kazepov, Y., 2020. Greening Vienna. The multi-level interplay of urban environmental policy-making. *Sustainability,* 12(4), p. 1577.

OekoBusinessWien, 2019. *Beste kommunale Daseinsvorsorge, € 695 Mio. Für moderne Öffis und € 64 Mio. Für noch mehr Grünraum im Kampf gegen den Klimawandel.* [online] Available at: https://bit.ly/3utNmMz [Accessed 02 April 2021].

Rechnungshof Österreich, 2005. *Wirkungsbereich der Bundeshauptstadt Wien-Prüfungsergebnisse: Stadtentwicklung und Stadtplanung.* [pdf] Available at: https://bit.ly/3fBcWL6 [Accessed 02 April 2021].

Riederer, B., Verwiebe, R. and Seewann, L., 2019. Changing social stratification in Vienna: Why are migrants declining from the middle of society? *Population, Space and Place,* 25(2), p. 2215.

Rode, P., & Schwab, E., 2017. Public green space in Vienna between utopia and political strategy. In: Hristova, S., and Czepczyński, M., eds., 2017. *Public space: between reimagination and occupation.* London: Routledge, pp. 147–157.

Rutt, R.L. and Gulsrud, N.M., 2016. Green justice in the city: A new agenda for urban green space research in Europe. *Urban Forestry & Urban Greening,* 19, pp. 123–127.

Sorensen, A., 2017. New institutionalism and planning theory. In: Gunder, M., Madanipour, A. and Watson, V., eds., 2017. *The Routledge handbook of planning theory.* London and New York: Routledge, pp. 250–263.

Statistik Austria. 2019. *Lohnsteuerpflichtige Einkommen nach Bezirken 2018—Frauen und Männer.* [online] Available at: https://bit.ly/2PNPPSW [Accessed 02 April 2021].

Suitner, J., 2020. Vienna's planning history: Periodizing stable phases of regulating urban development, 1820–2020. *Planning Perspectives,* pp. 1–22.

Walker, G., 2012. *Environmental justice: Concepts, evidence and politics.* London and New York: Routledge.

ZAMG-Klimaabteilung, 2019. *Klimatologische Kenntage in Wien 1955 bis 2019.* [online] Available at: https://bit.ly/3dwy4Qb [Accessed 02 April 2021].

9 Environmental quality for everyone? Socio-structural inequalities in mobility, access to green spaces and air quality

Michael Friesenecker, Bernhard Riederer and Roberta Cucca

Introduction

In the mid-1990s, urban planning approaches entered an era where sustainability goals, alongside the goal of climate protection, increasingly became woven into urban policy and planning (Wheeler, 2013). Initially conceptualised as a means of balancing environmental protection, social equality and economic growth, the sustainability concept was increasingly used by policymakers to emphasise, predominantly, the (smart) economic growth agenda (While et al., 2004). Whilst sustainability remains an important umbrella concept, more recently it has dovetailed with other concepts, such as the 'smart city', the 'resilient city' and the 'low-carbon city', to name a few (see de Jong et al., 2015). Beginning in 2010, the smart city concept became the new driving force for sustainable development. According to de Jong et al. (2015), the promotion of social inclusion and economic growth through digitalisation became distinctive features. More recently, the resilient city concept has emerged, with a focus on dampening the effects of climate change and other crises through adaption or introduction of green, grey and blue (water-related) urban infrastructure at finer spatial and temporal scales (Connolly, 2019).

Nevertheless, these policies have been met with severe criticism. There is evidence that greening strategies, intended or otherwise, might trigger the (re-)production of socio-spatial inequalities in access to environmental resources (Cucca, 2020). Connolly (2019), for instance, argues that the contemporary planning orthodoxy of the 'Smart Sustainable Resilient City' produces higher levels of social inequalities because planning policies often disregard questions of social equity. From this perspective, environmental improvements tend to

DOI: 10.4324/9781003133827-13

favour the already well-off, leading to gentrification, poverty and the displacement of the most vulnerable. Nevertheless, it very much depends on the context, especially with regard to differences between North America and Europe. Whilst the strong emphasis on public policies geared towards environmental improvements and enhancing the quality of life in European cities may deepen socio-spatial inequalities, these policies may also contain inequalities. In particular, Vienna has been praised for developing local housing policies that limit the rise of socio-spatial inequalities driven by urban greening and other environmental strategies (Anguelovski et al., 2018; Cucca, 2019).

Vienna's planning approach, which has traditionally focused on social equity and environmental protection, turned towards sustainability in the late 1990s, and this was further developed into a Smart City Strategy in 2014. With sustainability, economic development became equally as important as ecological and social concerns. Yet, Vienna pursued the delivery of its social and health-oriented key services to ensure healthy, liveable environments. Therefore, Vienna's status as a green city, characterised by high quality of life and excellent environmental quality, has not suffered. As such, Vienna has ranked amongst the highest performing European cities in relation to resident satisfaction with air quality, public transport, cleanliness and green spaces (Verwiebe et al., 2020, pp. 21–34).

Against this background, we examine Vienna's status as a liveable and green city more closely, with a particular emphasis on weighing up how 'just' it is. In doing so, we focus on different social groups' perceptions of environmental quality. Hence, our analysis seeks to answer the research questions: what is the extent of disparities in perceived environmental quality across social groups and how have these inequalities developed over time? Discussing the relationship between our findings and Vienna's environmental approach, we aim to explore possible social trade-offs and limitations of environmentally oriented policies.

In doing so, we draw on the concepts of recognitional and distributional justice, which have been central to the study of environmental justice (Schlosberg, 2007). The (lack of) recognition of group differences is conceptualised as an 'institutional practice' that may (re-)produce unequal distributional outcomes (ibid., p. 16; following the work of Nancy Fraser). In order to identify group differences, we use perceived environmental quality data for different social groups and housing areas to approximate distributional effects. We focus on the perception of space, measured through the satisfaction with environmental qualities, because it conditions people's use of space

Environmental quality for everyone? 133

and forms an important part of their daily lived realities (Merrifield, 1993, p. 524). However, as spatial-environmental policies have limited capabilities to improve the socio-economic conditions of individuals (Mouratidis, 2020), environmental policies should be understood as being complementary to a range of other policies, such as housing, welfare and labour market policies.

This chapter will proceed as follows: after outlining our analytical approach, we provide some context by describing Vienna's environmentally oriented policies, followed by a quantitative analysis of changes in perceived environmental quality of different social groups over time. In the concluding section, we will discuss the relation between (a) changes in environmentally oriented policies and (b) changes in perceived environmental quality in Vienna.

An analysis of Vienna's urban environmental justice

Our analytical approach was comprised of several steps: first, a qualitative analysis of policy documents and grey literature with the aim of identifying the most important reforms and instruments of Vienna's environmental policy approach since 1990. The documents and literature were thematically coded with a focus on social equity, especially if and how social disparities have been addressed through specific environmental improvements targeted at different social groups or housing areas.

Second, we analysed the distributional outcomes in terms of perceived environmental quality over time, employing data from the Viennese Quality of Life Survey for the years 2003, 2008, 2013 and 2018.[1] We constructed a perceived environmental quality index using information from five items within the questionnaire. Respondents evaluated (1) air quality, (2) road cleaning and (3) waste disposal in their living environment on a five-point scale (1= no problems, 5 = large problems). Furthermore, they reported their opinion on whether improvements are needed regarding the availability of (4) public transport and (5) green spaces, including courtyard greening (2003–2013: yes/no; 2018: five-point rating scale with 1 indicating highest relevance). The index counts the number of problems (values 3 to 5 on the first three items) and needs (yes answers 2003–2013, value 1 in 2018) regarding the living environment. It ranges from 0 (highest perceived quality) to 5 (lowest perceived quality).

Following a description of the changes in environmental quality, we ran a series of binary logistic regression models for 2003 and 2018 (no problems/needs vs. at least one). In these models, we examine the differences in perceived environmental quality across the dimensions of (a) labour market position, (b) equivalised net household income including welfare transfers (quantiles), (c) age groups, (d) gender (bivariate associations), (e) migration (country of birth in categories) and (f) housing areas (by the dominant type and age of buildings). The method proposed by Allison (1999) and Hoetker (2007) is applied to test whether the coefficients differ between the separately estimated models for 2003 and 2018, thus indicating changes in differences between social groups over time. Additionally, applying the KHB method (Karlson et al., 2012), we compared the group differences observed in the bivariate models for 2018 with the group differences in a multiple regression model for 2018 containing all variables (a)–(f) simultaneously. If a group difference is smaller in the multiple regression model than in the respective bivariate model, other variables account for it (indicating explanations for the initial group difference observed in the bivariate model). All main text tables show average marginal effects that were derived from the estimated regression models, which enhance the comparability of results stemming from different logistic models.

Vienna's environmental policy approach

Vienna stands out when it comes to key criteria for evaluating environmental justice. That is, according to a recent comparative investigation examining the urban greening policy trajectories of 50 cities in Europe, Canada and the United States over the last 25 years, its focus on health and equitable access to green infrastructures (Anguelovski et al., 2018). Aiming at social equity and a decent quality of life for all residents, the prime focus in Vienna has traditionally been on health, education and social welfare policies, including housing. This focus continues to be reflected in the budget plan of 2021: expenditures for social welfare and housing subsidies account for around 20% of the overall expenses, followed by 19% for both education and health.[2] Within this social and health-oriented focus, Vienna's environmental approach developed during the 1970s, when the newly founded *Department of Environmental Protection* and the *Department of Urban Planning* mainstreamed environmental concerns (Mocca et al., 2020). As a social-ecological approach to urban development, it centred around the notion of a 'healthy, liveable environment' contributing to, and improving the quality of life for Vienna's residents (Pirhofer and Stimmer, 2007, pp. 74–76). Services provided by the City – mainly public transport, green space, high-quality water supply, waste and resource management – are framed as socio-ecological key services which provide healthy environments whilst limiting environmental impacts at the same time.

During the 1990s, under the influence of international and EU environmental policies, Vienna's urban policy developed a stronger environmental orientation, with an emphasis on climate protection and the reduction of emissions. At the same time, sustainability came to be the leading principle in urban planning. Within the sustainability framework, economic development emerged as an important cornerstone in planning, equal to ecological and social concerns (see Chapter by 8 by Brenner et al. in this volume). This shift was made possible by decentralisation of the City's competences in regional economic and labour market policies, which were limited up until the 1990s (see Chapter 6 by Ahn and Kazepov in this volume). And it was justified by the City in light of Vienna's exposure to the inter-urban competition through Austria's accession to the EU. Facing the enlargement of the EU in 2004, the City saw the potential to position Vienna as a regional economic centre. Therefore, in the 2000s, Vienna started to market its social and ecological location qualities and services more prominently in order to strengthen Vienna's position as an important international business and research location (see Mocca et al., 2020, pp. 9–10).

Despite this shift towards branding and economic development, Vienna kept its commitment to its social and health-oriented key values and services. Waste management, water supply and road cleaning were never privatised and remained part of the administration, thus maintaining stable fees and high-quality services. Although energy provision and public transport were privatised in 1999 (Plank, 2020), the City retained full ownership of its transport operator and energy provider. As such, Vienna preserved the possibility of further shaping its socio-ecological approach. For example, the heating of social housing premises relies to a large degree on the use of cogeneration and waste incineration plants, which are equipped with a filtering technique to lower air pollution and greenhouse gases. Furthermore, existing social housing was retrofitted as a means of reducing emissions (Mocca et al., 2020).

Public transport represents another major social-ecological service in Vienna, as reflected in very high satisfaction scores (96%) compared to other European cities, such as London (88%), Stockholm (81%), Brussels (75%) or Lisbon (60%) (Verwiebe et al., 2020, p. 21). The local transport operator (*Wiener Linien*) remains heavily subsidised, enabling it to expand its network and improve its service by shortening headways and expanding the hours of service. Despite its privatisation in 1999, *Wiener Linien* has consistently received around 5% of the city's total expenditures per annum as subsidies,[2] cross-financed in part by revenue from parking space management (Buehler et al., 2016, p. 264). Most important for social equity and recognition was the introduction of a reduced fee for annual tickets. Campaigned as a 100€ ticket by the Green Party in the 2010 election, a 365€ ticket was finally introduced in coalition with the Social Democrats in 2012 (see Buehler et al., 2016 for details). Furthermore, the city's public transport approach also recognises the specific needs of some segments of the population, including the elderly, students and the socially excluded.

Yet, transport remains critical with regard to social and spatial disparities in environmental quality. The introduction of a new parking management system in 1993 (see again Buehler et al., 2016), accompanied by interventions in winter road clearance and the decrease of emission intensive fuel for heating in the beginning of the 2000s, led to a reduction in air pollution across most of the city (Kurz et al., 2014). Although car use for commuting to work fell from 38% in 2003 to 24% in 2018 (Verwiebe et al., 2020, p. 203), socio-spatial inequalities still exist between central and outer districts in terms of car-ownership, mobility behaviour and access to public transport (Haslauer et al., 2015; Bärnthaler et al., 2020). Furthermore, models by Kurz et al. (2014) clearly show that highways and main roads remain the main source of air pollution.

Finally, the preservation of green space is framed as another key feature contributing to quality of life for Vienna's residents. Around 50% of the city area is green space, though historic urbanisation patterns have led to uneven distribution and availability of green spaces (Haslauer et al., 2015). Satisfaction is high compared to other European cities, with 93% of the Viennese population reporting satisfaction with the provision of green space, compared to Barcelona (68%) and Amsterdam (89%) (Verwiebe et al., 2020). Influenced by increasing re-urbanisation of the inner-city district, the administration recognised an increasing need for the development and extension of green space during the 2000s. Furthermore, the experience of pronounced heatwaves led to a growing awareness of social disparities in the local provision of green and blue infrastructure, and their heightened effects on some members of the population, including the elderly, socially excluded and low-income residents (see Chapter 8 by Brenner et al. in this volume for more details).

Shifting to a Smart City Strategy in 2014, Vienna's focus on sustainability and enhancing quality of life through the provision of key services remained the underlying principles in its environmental policy

Environmental quality for everyone? 137

and urban planning. Although Vienna's environmental and social focus contrasts with stronger business and technology orientated smart city concepts, such as those of Barcelona or Berlin, innovation and technologies have become more important in linking economic development and environmental protection (Exner et al., 2018). Apart from responding to EU-related funding opportunities and branding Vienna as a business location, a major aim of the Smart City Strategy is to foster inter-departmental cooperation in climate protection policy (ibid.).

Socio-structural inequalities and perceived environmental quality

The above discussion has outlined Vienna's environmental approach and its main policy instruments, but also highlighted some criticisms in terms of uneven distribution of green space, air pollution and availability of public transport. In this section, we analyse perceived improvements in environmental quality and disparities between social groups. In so doing, we aim to grasp disparities in the lived experiences of different groups in relation to environmental qualities. This focus emphasises the importance of human-nature relations rather than solely focusing on improvements of the built environment. We first do this by considering the overall trends, and second by considering socio-demographic and spatial differences.

Overall, the perceived environmental quality in Vienna is high and has improved over time (see Figure 9.1): in 2018, 44% of the Viennese reported they did not have a single problem or need in relation to their living environment (72% reported at most one problem), compared to 36% in 2003 (68% reported at most one problem). Trends over time for single indicators of environmental quality are mixed. A need for green space, problems with air quality and problems with road cleaning were less often reported in 2018 compared to 15 years previous. Nevertheless, the need for additional green space remains the main concern of the Viennese (31% in 2003 and 26% in 2018). Problems with waste disposal were rarely reported and figures remained stable (~10%). In the growing city, however, only 18% reported the need for improved access to public transport in 2003 compared to 25% in 2018. Thus, reforms regarding the regulation of car traffic, for instance, seemed to be successful at meeting the perceived needs of residents whereas the population growth and development of new housing areas raised additional needs for a further expansion of public transport.

Whilst these findings are positive in general, there are pronounced differences in perceived environmental quality between social groups

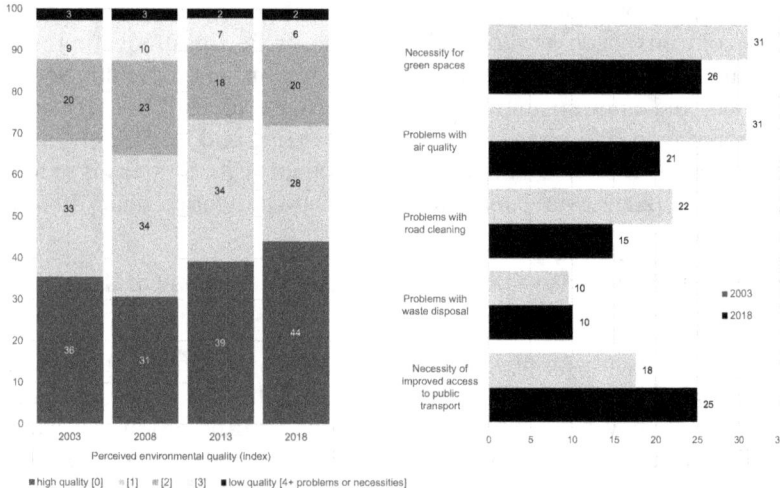

Figure 9.1 Perceived quality of the living environment in Vienna (in %).
Source: Viennese Quality of Life Survey 2003 to 2018; own weighted computation.
Note: Perceived environmental quality (0–5) is measured by counting reported problems with air quality, road cleaning and waste disposal and necessities of improvements in public transport and of additional green space.

(see Table 9.1). Perceived environmental quality differs by labour market position, household income, age, gender and country of birth. Whereas certain differences have remained constant (e.g. those relating to country of birth), some even increased between 2003 and 2018 (i.e. those by labour market position), leading to further social polarisation in perceived environmental quality, which supports the scepticism of some authors (Connolly, 2019; Cucca, 2020). Labour market position did not have much influence on the evaluation of the living environment in 2003. However, it has become highly relevant in 2018, when unskilled workers in particular, but also skilled workers, the unemployed and students showed lower probabilities of living in high-quality environments (see Table 9.1, 3rd column). Most of these differences are diminishing if other variables are included (see Table 9.1, 4th column), suggesting that effects of labour market position on the probability of living in high-quality environments partly result from differences in income and housing areas. Unsurprisingly, people with a lower household income have a lower probability of living in high-quality environments (see Table 9.1). Differences between income groups may be even more pronounced nowadays than in the past.[3]

Environmental quality for everyone? 139

Although there has been some change within groups, overall differences by age, gender and country of birth remained largely constant over time. According to Table 9.1, the share of those living in high-quality environments is more than 20 percentage points lower amongst the youngest (below age 30) than amongst the oldest age group (60+) in both 2003 and 2018. In line with this result, retired people report fewer problems or needs in relation to their living environment. These differences by age are partly explained by their labour market position, household income or housing area (compare third and fourth column in Table 9.1). An important aspect relates to restricted access to affordable housing for young newcomers to the city (see Kadi, 2015). In addition, women seem to be slightly underrepresented in high-quality living environments (differences of 2–3 percentage points), indicating that women who live alone have more difficulties in finding good housing (see Klinenberg, 2012). Finally, there is a pronounced difference between the European-born and the non-European-born population (Table 9.1). In the course of the last decades, the heterogeneity of the increasing immigration to Vienna affected social polarisation, with highly qualified immigrants from EU 15 member countries who have immediate access to the labour market and low-skilled immigrants from third countries as well as asylum seekers and refugees who suffer from legal obstacles (see Riederer et al., 2019, 2020). In 2018, immigrants from Turkey and other non-European countries were characterised as having lower probabilities of living in high-quality environments.[4] Differences in labour market position, household income and housing area account for a large part of their disadvantaged position (Table 9.1, 4th column). Presumably, weaker economic integration leads to lower income and non-affordability of high-quality living environments, but also discrimination and a lack of access to housing in high-quality environments for socio-economically weak newcomers, cause systematic disadvantages (see Kadi, 2015; Kohlbacher and Reeger, 2020).

Finally, findings on differences in housing areas[5] also mirror the general picture. The results reflect a general improvement of perceived quality of living environments, but also demonstrate differences between areas. People living in the city centre and surrounding neighbourhoods with buildings built in the period from 1840 to 1918 more frequently report problems than residents of other housing areas, in particular compared to those living in single-family homes (most of them at peripheral locations). Table 9.1 shows, for instance, that in 2003 the share reporting high environmental quality was about 21 percentage points higher amongst those living in single-family homes

Table 9.1 Regression models on perceived environmental quality

Average marginal effects (binary logistic regression models)	Lower vs. high environmental quality (0/1)		
	Bivariate	Bivariate	Multiple
	2003	2018	2018
Labour market position			
Liberal profession/freelancer	.00	.06	.05
Self-employed	.01	.09 *	.06
Higher employee	.06 **	.04	.00 z
Mid-level or lower	ref.	ref.	ref.
Skilled worker	.00	–.07 *	–.06 *
Unskilled worker	.03	–.20 ***	–.14 *** x
Unemployed	.02	–.06 *	–.02 y
Retired	.15 ***	.10 ***	.00 x
Students/in education	–.03	–.07 **	.03 x
Other (in leave etc.)	.01	–.14 ***	–.10 *** y
Cragg and Uhler's R^2	.03	.04 a	
Household income			
lowest quartile	–.03	–.14 ***	–.09 *** x
quartile 2	.00	–.06 **	–.04 y
quartile 3	ref.	ref.	ref.
highest quartile	.04 **	.04	.03
Cragg and Uhler's R^2	<.01	.02	
Age in years			
below 30	–.11 ***	–.16 ***	–.11 *** x
30–44	–.06 ***	–.08 ***	–.06 *** x
45–59	ref.	ref.	ref.
60+	.10 ***	.06 ***	.04

Cragg and Uhler's R^2	.04	.04 [b]	
Gender			
Male	ref.	ref.	ref.
Female	-.02 *	-.02	-.03 *
Cragg and Uhler's R^2	<.01	<.01	<.01
Country of birth			
Austria	ref.	ref.	ref.
Turkey	-.14 ***	-.13 ***	-.06 [x]
EU 15 (without AT)	-.01	.05	.05
Other European countries (non-EU 15)	-.01	-.02	.01 [z]
Other Non-European countries	-.02	-.14 ***	-.09 * [y]
Cragg and Uhler's R^2	<.01	.01	
Housing areas			
Single-family homes	.21 ***	.11 ***	.09 ***
City centre and buildings 1840–1918	ref.	ref.	ref.
Buildings 1918–1959	.16 ***	.05	.08 ** [z]
Buildings since 1960	.17 ***		
Buildings 1960–2000		.06 ***	.06 ***
Buildings since 2001		-.06 **	-.03 [z]
Unknown	.12 ***	-.05 **	.01 [x]
Cragg and Uhler's R^2	.04	.01 [a]	.07
N	8,228	8,088	8,088

Source: Viennese Quality of Life Survey 2003 and 2018; own weighted computation.

Notes: 'High environmental quality' is assumed if respondents did not report a single problem or need in relation to the living environment (see Figure 9.1). Average marginal effects show differences between the respective group and the reference group (ref.), where .02 means 2 p.p.; ***$p \leq .001$, **$p \leq .01$, *$p \leq .05$; change in bivariate effects (LR-Chi² test 2003 vs. 2018): [a]$p \leq .001$, [b]$p \leq .01$, [c]$p \leq .05$; change in coefficient if other variables included (KHB test for 2018): [x]$p \leq .001$, [y]$p \leq .01$, [z]$p \leq .05$.

than inner-city residents. Between 2003 and 2018, differences between housing areas have become smaller. This might be related to different lifestyles in the course of social upgrading (Hatz et al., 2016) but is most likely due to efforts in greening and traffic regulation: In 2003, 48% of inner-city residents reported a need for (additional) green space compared to 29% in 2018. Similar trends can be observed regarding problems with air quality (41 vs. 26%) and road cleaning (29 vs. 16%). At the periphery, problems are of a different nature: in 2018, 29% of those living in single-family homes expressed a need for improvements of public transport (2003: 34%). The latter is also an issue for 33% of the residents of new or renewed housing areas (data for 2018 only). In general, it seems that, due to declining differences between housing areas, neighbourhood effects are less important for Vienna than in the past.

Conclusions

In this chapter, we have analysed how the perception of Vienna's status as a green city has varied over time and across social groups. Furthermore, we aimed to explore how these changes relate to the shifting orientation of Vienna's social-environmental policies in order to discuss possible trade-offs and limitations of environmentally oriented policies.

In comparison to other European cities, the Viennese population is generally very satisfied with the city's environmental qualities. Furthermore, the perceived environmental quality has generally improved from what was already a high level, yet results show that pronounced inequalities exist. Whilst some of the differences remained stable over time, inequalities regarding the labour market position became more profound. Unskilled workers in particular perceive increased deficiencies in the quality of their environments. This seems to intersect with an ethnic dimension, as residents born in Turkey and other non-European countries face barriers on Vienna's labour and housing market. Nevertheless, inequalities between housing areas have fallen and in general the perceived environmental quality has improved but, unsurprisingly, problems with green space, air quality and public transport provision differ between inner-city housing and peripheral districts.

Along with the introduction of sustainability and the smart city concept, Vienna's focus on key services to provide healthy, liveable environments, whilst limiting environmental impacts continued on the whole. This commitment to providing key services mirrors a general improvement in the perceived environmental quality, although

Environmental quality for everyone? 143

the sustainable/smart approach was not able to iron out social disparities. With the addition of the economic growth agenda, mostly through locational branding and fostering environmental technologies, our evidence suggests that too little emphasis has been placed on addressing social inequalities in the provision of key services with environmental impacts.

Urban greening is less related to gentrification and displacement in Vienna in comparison to other contexts, and the existence of a good policy mix regarding affordability of housing largely limited inequalities. Nevertheless, when it comes to the lived experience of specific groups, the current situation of environmental justice should be taken seriously. The poorer provision of environmental quality to unskilled workers and the limited improvements for low-income residents in general may endanger the status of Vienna as a 'just' green city. Recent immigration and the associated barriers on the labour and housing markets for newcomers bring about challenges in providing environmental quality to everyone. The recent emergence of the resilience approach might strengthen the recognition of vulnerable groups, which has been so far limited in Vienna's environmental approach. However, it will succeed only if a good level of integration amongst different policy domains can be achieved.

Notes

1 The data is representative for the population of Vienna (age 15 and above) and includes information from 8,300 to 8,700 respondents each year. Interviews were conducted in German and in the mother tongue of the largest immigrant groups (i.e. those from Turkey and former Yugoslavia). Modes of data collection comprised computer assisted telephone interviews (all waves), face-to-face interviews (300 foreign language interviews, both in 2003 and 2008) and computer assisted web interviews (23% in 2018). Surveys were conducted by IFES (www.ifes.at) who weighted the data in consideration of design and mode effects.
2 The share of expenses remained stable according to the City's statement of accounts since 1998 (Source: https://bit.ly/3rEOb3h, Accessed 28 March 2021)
3 In 2003, 33% of the lowest and 40% of the highest income quantile reported no problems or needs concerning their living environment compared to 35% and 53% in 2018. However, differences between income groups in 2003 do not significantly differ from differences between income groups in 2018 (LR-Chi^2 test 2003 vs. 2018; Table 9.1).
4 In 2003, 23% of Turkish immigrants but 34% of EU 15 immigrants reported no problems or needs in relation to their living environment. In 2018, these figures refer to 32% and 50%, respectively.
5 The classification on housing areas is based on construction period and quality of the housing stock. See Riederer et al. (2019, p.4) for details.

References

Allison, P.D., 1999. Comparing logit and probit coefficients across groups. *Sociological Methods & Research*, 28(2), pp. 186–208.

Anguelovski, I., Argüelles, L., Baró, F., Cole, H., Connolly, J., García Lamarca, M., Loveless, S., Pulgar, C., Shokry, G., Trebic, T. and Wood, E., 2018. Green trajectories: Municipal policy trends and strategies for greening in Europe, Canada and United States (1999–2016). Available at: https://bit.ly/3sIobVK [Accessed 31 March 2021]

Bärnthaler, R., Novy, A. and Stadelmann, B., 2020. A Polanyi-inspired perspective on social-ecological transformations of cities, *Journal of Urban Affairs*, pp. 1–25. https://doi.org/10.1080/07352166.2020.1834404.

Buehler, R., Pucher, J. and Altshuler, A., 2017. Vienna's path to sustainable transport, *International Journal of Sustainable Transportation*, 11(4), pp. 257–271.

Connolly, J.J., 2019. From Jacobs to the Just City: A foundation for challenging the green planning orthodoxy. *Cities* 91, pp. 64–70.

Cucca, R., 2019. Taking contextual differences into account in green gentrification research. The case of Vienna. *Sociologia urbana e rurale*, 119, pp. 46–62.

Cucca, R., 2020. Spatial segregation and the quality of the local environment in contemporary cities. In: Musterd, S., ed., 2020. *Handbook of urban segregation*. Cheltenham: Edward Elgar Publishing. pp. 185–199.

de Jong, M., Joss, S., Schraven, D., Zhan, C. and Weijnen, M., 2015. Sustainable–smart–resilient–low carbon–eco–knowledge cities: Making sense of a multitude of concepts promoting sustainable urbanization. *Journal of Cleaner Production*, 109, pp. 25–38.

Exner, A., Cepoiu, L., Weinzierl, C. and Asara, V., 2018. Performing smartness differently-strategic enactments of a global imaginary in three European cities. *SRE – Discussion Papers* 2018/05. WU Vienna University of Economics and Business, Vienna. Available at: https://bit.ly/39uGBSC [Accessed 31 March 2021]

Haslauer, E., Delmelle, E.C., Keul, A., Blaschke, T. and Prinz, T., 2015. Comparing subjective and objective quality of life criteria: A case study of green space and public transport in Vienna, Austria. *Social Indicators Research*, 124(3), pp. 911–927.

Hatz, G., Kohlbacher, J. and Reeger, U., 2016. Socio-economic segregation in Vienna: A social-oriented approach to urban planning and housing. In: Tammaru, T., Marcinczak, S., van Ham, M. and Musterd, S., eds., 2016. *Socio-economic segregation in European capital cities: East meets west*. London: Routledge, pp. 80–109.

Hoetker, G., 2007. The use of logit and probit models in strategic management research: Critical issues. *Strategic Management Journal*, 28(4), pp. 331–343.

Kadi, J., 2015. Recommodifying housing in formerly "Red" Vienna? *Housing, Theory and Society*, 32(3), pp. 247–65.

Karlson, K.B., Holm, A. and Breen, R., 2012. Comparing regression coefficients between same-sample nested models using logit and probit: A new method. *Sociological Methodology*, 42(1), pp. 286–313.

Klinenberg, E., 2012. *Going solo. The extraordinary rise and surprising appeal of living alone.* New York: The Penguin Press.
Kohlbacher, J. and Reeger, U., 2020. Globalization, immigration and ethnic diversity: The exceptional case of Vienna. In: Musterd, S., ed., 2020. *Handbook of urban segregation.* Cheltenham: Edward Elgar Publishing, pp. 101–117.
Kurz, C., Orthofer, R., Sturm, P., Kaiser, A., Uhrner, U., Reifeltshammer, R. and Rexeis, M, 2014. Projection of the air quality in Vienna between 2005 and 2020 for NO_2 and PM10. *Urban Climate*, 10, pp. 703–719.
Merrifield, A., 1993. Place and space: A Lefebvrian reconciliation. *Transactions – Institute of British Geographers*, 18(4), pp. 516–531.
Mocca, E., Friesenecker, M. and Kazepov, Y., 2020. Greening Vienna. The multi-level interplay of urban environmental policy-making. *Sustainability*, 12(4), pp. 1–18. https://doi.org/10.3390/su12041577.
Mouratidis, K., 2020. Neighborhood characteristics, neighborhood satisfaction, and well-being: The links with neighborhood deprivation. *Land Use Policy*, 99, pp. 1–12. https://doi.org/10.1016/j.landusepol.2020.104886
Pirhofer, G. and Stimmer, K., 2007. *Pläne für Wien. Theorie und Praxis der Wiener Stadtplanung von 1945 bis 2005.* Vienna: Municipal Department 18, City of Vienna.
Plank, L., 2019. Öffentliche Dienste weiter denken: Internationale Erfahrungen für Wien. In: Plank, L., Hamedinger, A. and Novy, A., eds., 2019. *Wien – Ein Modell im Zukunftstest.* Wien: Kurswechsel, pp. 45–52.
Riederer, B., Buber-Ennser, I. and Haindorfer, R., 2020. Trends in demography and migration in Austria. In: Tálas, P. and Etl, A., eds., 2020. *Demography and migration in Central and Eastern Europe.* Budapest: Dialog Campus Publishing, pp. 9–27.
Riederer, B., Verwiebe, R. and Seewann, L., 2019. On changing social stratification in Vienna: Why are migrants declining from the middle of society? *Population, Space and Place*, 25(2), pp. 1–11. https://doi.org/10.1002/psp.2215
Schlosberg, D., 2007. *Defining environmental justice: Theories, movements, and nature.* Oxford: Oxford University Press.
Verwiebe, R., Haindorfer, R., Dorner, J., Liedl, B. and Riederer, B., 2020. *Lebensqualität in einer wachsenden Stadt: Wiener Lebensqualitätsstudie 2018. Werkstattbericht 187.* Vienna: Stadt Wien, Stadtentwicklung und Stadtplanung.
Wheeler, S.M., 2013. *Planning for sustainability: Creating livable, equitable and ecological communities.* London: Routledge.
While, A., Jonas, A.E. and Gibbs, D., 2004. The environment and the entrepreneurial city: searching for the urban 'sustainability fix' in Manchester and Leeds. *International Journal of Urban and Regional Research*, 28(3), pp. 549–569.

10 Vienna's resilience

Between urban justice and the challenges ahead

Roland Verwiebe, Yuri Kazepov, Michael Friesenecker and Byeongsun Ahn

Introduction

In the past, Vienna and other metropolises (such as Amsterdam, Berlin, Barcelona, Copenhagen and Stockholm) have been regarded as prime examples of the *European city* model (Le Galès, 2002; Häussermann, 2005). However, trajectories of European cities have increasingly diversified over the last 30 years as a result of varied reactions to a broad set of transformations. These transformations include the following: de-industrialisation and the consequent changing occupational structure (Hamnett, 2021); welfare rescaling (Kazepov and Barberis, 2017); growing inequality (Cucca and Ranci, 2017); housing shortages (Scanlon et al., 2014); broader demographic changes (Kreichauf, 2018; Wolff and Wiechmann, 2018); a fragmentation of the political (party) system (Ford and Jennings, 2020); efforts to govern climate change and environmental risks (Kern, 2019; Bulkeley, 2021); and, more recently, the economic and social consequences of the financial crises of 2008 and the COVID-19 pandemic (Hadjimichalis, 2011; Guida and Carpentieri, 2021). Yet, many scholars agree that the starting point for the process of differentiation among European cities is located in the post-Fordist transformation (Amin, 1995). This does not mean that differences did not exist before (see Diefendorf, 1989). On the contrary, it means that differences have been superseded by economic growth (unequally distributed, but existing, nonetheless) and Keynesian state intervention that attempted to iron them out (Brenner, 2004). The crisis of Fordism, despite the accompanying spread of an all-encompassing neoliberal narrative, brought about differentiated patterns of demographic change (with rising migration) and economic development (often with jobless growth) that began reshaping the social fabric of European cities. These changes challenged the balance between economic competitiveness and social cohesion that had once characterised the system of governance, exposing urban economies to rising inequalities

DOI: 10.4324/9781003133827-14

and emerging social polarisation (Cucca and Ranci, 2017). As a result, growth-oriented policy agendas reinforced the unequal distribution of the costs of transition to the new patterns, and these were paralleled by a retrenchment of welfare state provision. While some scholars attribute this development to the overall process of neoliberalisation drawing cities into its orbit (Harvey, 2005; Mayer, 2007), in this volume we have a more nuanced perspective. Neoliberalism does indeed affect European cities, but we see urban change as a more complex and localised outcome of a (partly) path-dependent process in which the distinctive institutional and structural contexts play a significant role – not only in filtering global processes but also in shaping the ways in which they play out (Musterd and Ostendorf, 1998; Fainstein, 2010; Andreotti et al., 2018).

Embracing this approach, each chapter of this volume analyses how Vienna's institutions have been challenged by the changes taking place, and how they have reacted. More specifically, they do so across four major policy fields – political participation, housing, labour market and environmental sustainability – attempting to better understand how the transformations have changed the degree of inclusiveness of the city, as well as resulting patterns of social justice. They identify potential trade-offs, negative synergic effects and dualisation trends that have emerged since the early 1990s. Indeed, notwithstanding the mediating role of Vienna's existing redistributive system (both cash and in-kind), evidence from the chapters of this volume point to growing vulnerabilities among different social groups and widening urban inequalities, on the one hand; and putting the City of Vienna under pressure to innovate their policy-making system, on the other. By investigating multiple policy dimensions, the authors have carried out an analysis of policy changes embedded in the interplay between institutional actors across different territorial jurisdictions. These changes have had variegated effects, sometimes simultaneously reinforcing the inclusion of certain groups and the exclusion of others. The following section highlights the major findings of the volume, addressing structural constraints and social innovation cross-cutting the various policy domains characterising Vienna's institutional landscape, highlighting how they are reshaping the boundaries of social justice.

Between resilience and change: key findings of the volume

The analyses of the four policy areas provide important insights and details about the process through which inclusion and exclusion occur and are consolidated. Not all social groups are affected, or are affected in the same way, but for some, these processes lead to culminating disadvantage.

Mocca and Friesenecker (Chapter 2), and Ahn and Mocca (Chapter 3) discuss the changing practices of *political participation* and governance structures in Vienna. Mocca and Friesenecker start out with an analysis of how the Social Democratic Party of Austria (SPÖ) were able to hold on to the mayoral office from 1919 to the present day (with a short exception during the Nazi regime), through widespread consensus, thanks to its generous redistributive policies and the provision of key public services. Thus, they have effectively maintained unparalleled, long-standing political control over the city. However, the rise of smaller parties in recent elections (such as the Greens; the liberal party, NEOS; and the right-wing Freedom Party of Austria (FPÖ)) indicates an emerging differentiation of the party spectrum. Similar to other European cities (Rontos et al., 2016; Eizaguirre et al., 2017; Russell, 2019), new political cleavages have emerged in Vienna. These social or spatial cleavages in voting might be the result of the vulnerabilities that globalisation and economic restructuring have kicked off. This has led to the *Green-Alternative-Liberal vs. Traditional-Authoritarian-Nationalist divide*, associated with transborder mobility and the economic integration of the European Union (Ford and Jennings, 2020). As Ahn and Mocca show in their analysis, despite innovation in the party system and the emergence of new political cleavages, political participation in the city is situated in the context of a *top-down* governing system and a strong legacy of vertical policy-making (Brandtner et al., 2017). However, from the early 1970s onwards, the City of Vienna has established a diverse range of participatory tools to encourage bottom-up mobilisation of community-based initiatives. A parallel process of decentralisation in the city has shifted power and resources to public enterprises and district authorities, opening up additional participatory pathways – albeit limited to small-scale urban planning. While opportunities for citizen participation have improved, bureaucratic obstacles have simultaneously increased (Brait and Hammer, 2017), resulting in an uneven distribution of participatory channels across the city which favours inner-city districts, where educational attainment and median earnings are higher. This policy deficit hinders a meaningful involvement of citizens from the lower social classes (e.g. in American and British cities, see Taylor, 2007; van Holm, 2019).

In the section on *housing* (Chapters 4 and 5), Litschauer and Friesenecker discuss key aspects of the transformation of Vienna's housing model and how it has come under pressure over the last three decades. However, contrary to other European cities, such as Amsterdam,

Berlin or Dublin (Adelhof et al., 2008; Tsenkova and Polanska, 2014; Byrne and Norris, 2019; Granath Hansson and Lundgren, 2019), the authors acknowledge that social housing still remains the largest housing segment in Vienna, providing affordable housing to roughly 40% of the city's population with the aim of avoiding segregation. This has been accomplished through: (1) massive investment in the maintenance of the existing public housing stock; (2) increased construction of subsidised social housing, mainly built by limited-profit housing associations to ensure below-market rent vis-à-vis high construction quality for its tenants; (3) targeting social housing, not only at the poor, but also offering options for the middle classes through high-income thresholds; (4) an active land banking and zoning policy that guarantees plots for the construction of new affordable housing; (5) quality management that ensures social orientation (e.g. affordability) and housing quality for new, large-scale, constructions. Nevertheless, the past decades have also seen liberalising tendencies of the Austrian federal government reduce the distributive effects of rent regulation in the private rental segment, leading to steep price increases and the rise of time-limited rental contracts (Kadi, 2015). These developments have also affected the redistributive capacity of social housing. Municipal housing has become more socially targeted, while escalating land prices, changing housing needs due to ageing, immigration and climate change pose further challenges in the provision of new social housing to low-income groups (Scanlon et al., 2014). In a nutshell, Vienna's housing system has witnessed an evolving insider-outsider divide between the social and private rental segments, and within the private rental segment, corresponding to the duration of one's residency in Vienna. In both segments, sitting tenants enjoy affordable and secure housing, while conversely, housing becomes less affordable to newcomers (especially low-income groups, low-skilled immigrants and refugees), who also face increasing housing insecurity.

The section on *labour transformations* (Chapters 6 and 7) delves into changes in the labour market and the role of Vienna's regulatory autonomy in mediating local outcomes of structural transformations (Österle and Heitzmann, 2020). In Chapter 6, Ahn and Kazepov point out that the long-standing institutional capacity development has enabled the city administration to mobilise effectively against the restrictive reform strategies of the federal government, providing more generous benefits and innovative employment programs for increasingly vulnerable social groups. For example, Vienna's regional minimum income scheme – despite federal reform attempts – continues to provide asylum seekers with access to employment services, which is not the case in other parts of Austria (Rathgeb, 2021). This local welfare system has been crucial in mediating tertiarisation, professionalisation and polarisation tendencies that currently unfold in Vienna. These are leading to new forms of social inequalities that Riederer, Verwiebe and Ahn describe, in Chapter 7, as *asymmetrical polarisation* (for international comparisons, see Crankshaw, 2017; Hamnett, 2021). While substantial growth in the class of professionals and managers has been a dominating trend, growing inequalities and a parallel polarisation of the occupational class structure cannot be neglected. For example, an increasing share of younger workers and educated women holding professional and managerial positions tend to be employed on a part-time and/or temporary basis, thus showing more vulnerability (Riederer and Berghammer, 2020). There is also a parallel and increasing polarisation within the migrant population. Labour migrants from the 1960s and 1970s and other long-term migrants suffer from higher shares of unemployment and social decline, whereas more recent immigrants – especially those from EU-15 countries – tend, on average, to be even more successful on the Viennese labour market than Austrian citizens.

In the section on *the environment*, Brenner, Mocca, and Friesenecker (Chapter 8) and Friesenecker, Riederer, and Cucca (Chapter 9) analyse environmental justice and sustainability. Brenner et al. argue that, compared to other cities (Anguelovski et al., 2018), Vienna has maintained a high share of Urban Green Space (UGS) (encompassing around 50% of the city) because of its strong state-based approach. This has made it possible for the City to react to structural challenges, including population growth, increasing inequalities, heatwaves and changing weather conditions. Support also came from higher levels, such as the EU, which introduced new opportunities for stronger environmental protection, while public sector maintenance of green spaces is outstanding and stands in contrast to an international trend towards more market-oriented UGS management (Rutt and Gulsrud, 2016; Kronenberg et al., 2020). According to Friesenecker et al., the (semi) public provision of key environmental services for healthy and liveable environments also include public transportation, water supply, waste management and energy, to name only the most important. While this continuous provision of services has contributed to Vienna's reputation as one of the most liveable and green cities in Europe (Verwiebe et al., 2020), the authors reveal that some citizens, especially unskilled workers and migrants, increasingly perceive the environment to be of a lower quality, especially in densely populated, lower income neighbourhoods with a higher share of immigrants. This corresponds to small pockets of undersupply in UGS, while access to an adequate amount of green space is ensured for the vast majority of the population. Furthermore, disparities between central and peripheral city areas exist, particularly concerning prevalent problems with green space, air quality and the provision of public transport. While environmental policies in Vienna are less related to gentrification and displacement compared to other cities (Anguelovski et al., 2018), the authors of both chapters argue that (perceived) inequalities in accessing environmentally friendly services and healthy, liveable environments at the neighbourhood level should be taken seriously. Particular attention should be paid to climate change associated heat waves and its health impacts for the elderly and socially deprived population, which will be key future challenges for environmental justice and sustainability in Vienna.

Vienna's emerging vulnerabilities

In light of the growing tendency towards market-led urban development models across cities and regions, scholars in the field of planning have invoked the notion of urban justice, proposing a conceptual framework for evaluating the social effects of neoliberal urban policies and practices (Marcuse et al., 2009; Fainstein, 2010; Knijn and Lepianka, 2020; Moroni, 2020). Accordingly, Fainstein (2014) proposes that the three governing principles for urban justice include *democracy*, *diversity* and *equity*, which form the rhetoric around urban policy, shaping the quality of urban life. These governing principles aim at promoting urban justice within the broader governance system, advocating greater political representation of non-elite interests regarding cultural recognition and economic redistribution (Fraser, 2009). Consequently, achieving meaningful, democratic outcomes in urban policy-making requires a transversal approach to planning, connecting different policy dimensions of institutional justice, on the one hand; and fostering the inclusion of diverse social groups and their interests by redrawing the boundaries of social justice, on the other hand.

The authors of this volume have addressed how post-Fordist transformation in Vienna has affected the three criteria of justice, cross-cutting the city's four major policy fields – political participation, housing, the labour market and the environment. While observing some trade-offs between economic competitiveness and social cohesion in recent years, their conclusions point out that existing regulatory frameworks for Vienna's urban institutions continue to play a strategic role in mitigating the repercussions of external crises. Strong governmental intervention in the key policy arenas characterises the particular political dimension of Vienna's urban justice, rooted in its top-down policy-making style, mediating the contradictory effect of the deliberative approach to planning that may reinforce the exclusion of disadvantaged social groups. Strong governmental intervention has been particularly successful in urban development and affordable housing provision, linking its formal policy-making structure to the needs of the broader society (i.e. not just the needy), on the one hand; and limiting the potential interference of market actors, on the other. Regarding the redistributive dimension of urban justice, Vienna's local welfare system remains strong and crucial for the protection of emerging vulnerable populations. Drawing on the autonomy acquired as a consequence of the long-standing decentralisation and institutional capacity it developed, the City of Vienna was able to implement need-oriented policies that addressed urban problems, as well as complementing federal policies with the provision of its own active labour market policies and social housing. This institutional innovation has created *just* access to public services and benefits, and has promoted social inclusion and diversity in community-oriented urban development.

Notwithstanding these institutional capabilities, however, the authors have also identified some exclusionary tendencies in the four policy areas, fuelling socio-economic vulnerability. This is particularly true for non-EU migrants, young people and low-income households. In fact, despite the generous local welfare system, Vienna's transition into an innovation-driven urban economy has engendered a new division of labour, segmenting a large proportion of the city's migrant population into low-wage and low-skill occupations. Currently, this trend towards polarisation among non-EU migrants coincides with the professionalisation of highly skilled EU-15 migrants and the decline of migrant middle classes. Although less pronounced, a series of recent housing reforms have also changed the eligibility criteria for affordable social housing, widening the gap between newcomers and sitting tenants. While continuing the *housing for all* approach, the impact of demographic change has placed new challenges on the right to housing, aggravating housing inequality among low-income households. Paradoxically, these challenges are emerging amid growing opportunities for grassroots participation in urban policy-making, especially in small-scale urban planning and subsidised social housing. In line with Fainstein's (2010, 2014) criticism of the popular demand for deliberative democracy, the current trend in Vienna's urban politics nuances equitable urban development, which is increasingly at odds with democratic principles of political participation, failing to ensure adequate representation of diverse local interests. This changing policy context may have emerged (in part) from the transformation of needs, claims and demands of Vienna's growing population, featured by the declining working-class dominance and the widening barriers of electoral participation for migrants in urban politics. These changes produce new vulnerabilities, necessitating a new innovative turn in urban policy-making.

Vienna, a *just city* of the 21st century? Challenges for future urban development

If Vienna wants to remain a *just city*, with a high degree of inclusiveness, it must address several challenges, ranging from persistent (low but rising) structural inequalities to demographic transitions, from climate change to digitalisation and multi-level governance. These challenges do not pertain to a single dimension, but cut across the whole urban social fabric.

Social inequalities as a challenge

As the chapters in this book have documented, inequalities are on the rise and remain one of the key challenges for urban futures. Economic and labour market restructuring processes produce new socio-economic divides and vulnerabilities that bring about an increase of people at-risk of poverty and living in precarious financial situations (Verwiebe et al., 2020). In this regard, trends of digitalisation will further impact Vienna's service-oriented labour market in the coming years. Here, much depends on Vienna's ability to create local jobs and invest in future technologies, ecology and digitalisation, addressing the gap between low and high qualified labour force. Vienna's current urban development strategies (e.g. Smart City Strategy) is a promising way into the future, going beyond a mere technological approach and embracing social inclusion targets. Yet, the great challenge relates to how social policies can be innovated beyond active labour market approaches, focusing on educational training and investments. Raising low incomes in specific branches (e.g. through minimum income schemes and the reduction of precarious jobs) will be the basis upon which to build more empowering and capacity-building policies. The feasibility of such policies depends on the future availability of financial resources which, in view of the city's growing budget deficit, points to an additional challenge that Vienna needs to address.

The challenge of dualisation

The future redistributive capacity of Vienna's housing model will also depend, to a large extent, on how labour market and social policies might interrupt the trends of dualisation and socio-spatial inequalities over the coming years. This is true despite the fact that eligibility criteria for a large proportion of municipal housing stock and parts of the new subsidised stock have become targeted at the inclusion of vulnerable groups, as well as including parts of the (increasingly precarious) middle classes (Friesenecker and Kazepov, 2021). Continuous investment in maintaining old (and building new) social housing each year, as well as recent reforms countering neoliberal tendencies, will potentially strengthen the redistributive capacity of the City's housing model (Kadi et al., 2021). However, this capacity will diminish, especially in combination with population growth (+350,000 inhabitants over the last 20 years: https://bit.ly/2TjOlS7), and diversifying housing needs. Moreover, policies geared at liberalisation and financialisation of the private housing segment need to be countered, especially at the federal and European level, highlighting the multi-level governance strategies that the city should expand.

The climate change challenge

Another key challenge, cutting across all policy themes, relates to the climate crisis. Countering social and spatial inequalities is a key issue for an environmentally *just city*. The city is in a strong position when it comes to providing public infrastructure that combines social and ecological aspects (Bärnthaler et al., 2020). The ability to control key services (such as water and energy production, the public transportation system, the housing sector and city planning) through public ownership in times of austerity and increasing public debt play a crucial role in countering socio-spatial inequalities. In view of this, measures to increase the participation (but also responsibility) of citizens in co-creating their local environments also represent promising ways towards a more inclusive and *just city*. This also implies addressing inequalities in accessing environmentally friendly infrastructure, including green space. This became crucial during the COVID-19 pandemic but is also a key challenge in countering the exposure to environmental harms, such as the effects of heatwaves on elderly and the socially deprived population.

The challenge of participation in multi-level governance

These emerging challenges resonate with another key challenge for the future, which is maintaining political participation in complex multi-level governance arrangements. One example of how this challenge plays out at the *horizontal* level is in regard to integrating the growing numbers of the population who are excluded from voting. Indeed, the internationalisation of the city has increased the *electoral gap*: 30% of the Viennese population are ineligible to vote because they do not have citizenship. Moreover, among eligible voters, turnout rates decreased and protest votes increased (especially among the working class). While Vienna has developed its repertoire of participatory processes, at least at the neighbourhood level, spatial inequalities and uneven social patterns in participatory processes limit the ability to address shortcomings in representative democracy. In order to close the electoral and participatory gap, there is a need for an improvement in the inclusion of the foreign-born and immigrant populations in civil society associations and political and administrative offices. An example of how the challenge plays out along the *vertical* dimension of multi-level governance relates to the City's capacity to politically counteract ongoing welfare retrenchments and neoliberal oriented policies. Increased efforts to build broader political alliances between Austrian and European cities, and rebuilding solidarity among federal states beyond party interests, NGOs and civil society associations, will be crucial in transforming the upper-tier levels towards complementary multi-level arrangements that focus on improving the living conditions of residents, and reducing inequalities.

Such challenges are common to most European cities; the existing institutional infrastructure in Vienna and its resilience provide a good starting point from which to address them. Will the city be willing to take on the challenge?

References

Adelhof, K., Glock, B., Lossau, J. and Schulz, M., eds., 2008. *Urban trends in Berlin and Amsterdam*. Berlin: Berliner Geographische Arbeiten.

Amin, A., ed., 1995. *Post-Fordism: A reader*. Hoboken, NJ: John Wiley & Sons Ltd.

Andreotti, A., Benassi, D. and Kazepov, Y., eds., 2018. *Western capitalism in transition: Global processes, local challenges*. Manchester: Manchester University Press.

Anguelovski, I., Connolly, J.J.T., Masip, L., et al., 2018. Assessing green gentrification in historically disenfranchised neighborhoods: A longitudinal and spatial analysis of Barcelona. *Urban Geography*, 39(3), pp. 458–491.

Bärnthaler, R., Novy, A. and Stadelmann, B., 2020. A Polanyi-inspired perspective on social-ecological transformations of cities. *Journal of Urban Affairs*, online first: doi 10.1080/07352166.2020.1834404.

Brait, R. and Hammer, K., 2017. The Viennese Grätzloase the role of the commons in countering market-based transformations of the city. *Der Öffentliche Sektor - The Public Sector*, 43(1), pp. 33–43. https://doi.org/10.34749/OES.2017.2375

Brandtner, C., Höllerer, M.A., Meyer, R.E., et al., 2017. Enacting governance through strategy: A comparative study of governance configurations in Sydney and Vienna. *Urban Studies*, 54(5), pp. 1075–1091.

Brenner, N., 2004. *New state spaces: Urban governance and the rescaling of statehood*. Oxford: Oxford University Press.

Bulkeley, H., 2021. Climate changed urban futures: Environmental politics in the anthropocene city. *Environmental Politics*, 30(1–2), pp. 226–284.

Byrne, M. and Norris, M., 2019. Housing market financialization, neoliberalism and everyday retrenchment of social housing. *Environment and Planning A: Economy and Space*. https://doi.org/10.1177/0308518X19832614

Crankshaw, O., 2017. Social polarization in global cities: Measuring changes in earnings and occupational inequality. *Regional Studies*, 51(11), pp. 1612–1621.

Cucca, R. and Ranci, C., 2017. *Unequal cities: The challenge of post-industrial transition in times of austerity*. London and New York: Routledge.

Diefendorf, J.M., 1989. Urban reconstruction in Europe after World War II. *Urban Studies*, 26, pp. 128–143.

Eizaguirre, S., Pradel-Miquel, M. and García, M., 2017. Citizenship practices and democratic governance: 'Barcelona en Comú' as an urban citizenship confluence promoting a new policy agenda. *Citizenship Studies*, 21(4), pp. 425–439.

Fainstein, S., 2010. *The just city*. Ithaca, NY: Cornell University Press.

Fainstein, S., 2014. The just city. *International Journal of Urban Sciences*, 18(1), pp. 1–18.

Ford, R. and Jennings, W., 2020. The changing cleavage politics of Western Europe. *Annual Review of Political Science*, 23(1), pp. 295–314.

Fraser, N., 2009. *Scales of justice: Reimagining political space in a globalizing world*. New York: Columbia University Press.

Friesenecker, M. and Kazepov, Y., 2021. Housing Vienna: The socio-spatial effects of inclusionary and exclusionary mechanisms of housing provision. *Social Inclusion*, 9(2), pp. 77–90.

Granath Hansson, A. and Lundgren, B., 2019. Defining social housing: A discussion on the suitable criteria. *Housing, Theory and Society*, 36(2), pp. 149–166.

Guida, C. and Carpentieri, G., 2021. Quality of life in the urban environment and primary health services for the elderly during the Covid-19 pandemic: An application to the city of Milan (Italy). *Cities (London, England)*, 110, p. 103038.

Hadjimichalis, C., 2011. Uneven geographical development and socio-spatial justice and solidarity: European regions after the 2009 financial crisis. *European Urban and Regional Studies*, 18(3), pp. 254–274.

Hamnett, C., 2021. The changing social structure of global cities: Professionalisation, proletarianisation or polarisation. *Urban Studies,* 58(5), pp. 1050–1066.
Harvey, D., 2005. *A brief history of neoliberalism.* Oxford: Oxford University Press.
Häussermann, H., 2005. The end of the European City? *European Review,* 13(2), pp. 237–249.
Kadi, J., 2015. Recommodifying housing in formerly "Red" Vienna? *Housing, Theory and Society,* 32(3), pp. 247–265.
Kadi, J., Vollmer, L. and Stein, S., 2021. Post-neoliberal housing policy? Disentangling recent reforms in New York, Berlin and Vienna. *European Urban and Regional Studies.* https://doi.org/10.1177/09697764211003626
Kazepov, Y. and Barberis, E., 2017. The territorial dimension of social policies and the new role of cities. In: Lendvai-Bainton, N. and Kennett, P., eds., 2017. *Handbook of European social policy:* Cheltenham and Northampton, MA: Edward Elgar Publishing, pp. 302–318.
Kern, K., 2019. Cities as leaders in EU multilevel climate governance: Embedded upscaling of local experiments in Europe. *Environmental Politics,* 28(1), pp. 125–145.
Knijn, T. and Lepianka, D., 2020. *Justice and vulnerability in Europe: An interdisciplinary approach.* Cheltenham, UK and Northampton, MA: Edward Elgar Publishing Limited.
Kreichauf, R., 2018. From forced migration to forced arrival: The campization of refugee accommodation in European cities. *Comparative Migration Studies,* 6(1), p. 7.
Kronenberg, J., Haase, A., Łaszkiewicz, E., et al., 2020. Environmental justice in the context of urban green space availability, accessibility, and attractiveness in postsocialist cities. *Cities,* 106, p. 102862.
Le Galès, P., 2002. *European cities: Social conflicts and governance.* Oxford: Oxford University Press.
Marcuse, P., Connolly, J., Novy, J., et al., eds., 2009. *Searching for the just city: Debates in urban theory and practice.* London and New York: Routledge.
Mayer, M., 2007. Contesting the neoliberalization of urban governance. In: Leitner, H., Peck, J. and Sheppard, E.S., eds., 2007. *Contesting neoliberalism: Urban frontiers.* New York: Guilford Press, pp. 90–115.
Moroni, S., 2020. The just city. Three background issues: Institutional justice and spatial justice, social justice and distributive justice, concept of justice and conceptions of justice. *Planning Theory,* 19(3), pp. 251–267.
Musterd, S. and Ostendorf, W., 1998. *Urban segregation and the welfare state: Inequality and exclusion in Western cities.* London: Routledge.
Österle, A. and Heitzmann, K., 2020. Austrification in welfare system change? An analysis of welfare system development in Austria between 1998 and 2018. In: Blum, S., Kuhlmann, J. and Schubert, K., eds., 2020. *Routledge handbook of European welfare systems.* London and New York: Routledge, Taylor & Francis Group, pp. 21–37.

Rathgeb, P., 2021. Makers against takers: The socio-economic ideology and policy of the Austrian Freedom Party. *West European Politics,* 44(3), pp. 635–660.

Riederer, B. and Berghammer, C., 2020. The part-time revolution: Changes in the parenthood effect on women's employment in Austria across the birth cohorts from 1940 to 1979. *European Sociological Review,* 36(2), pp. 284–302.

Rontos, K., Grigoriadis, E., Sateriano, A., et al., 2016. Lost in protest, found in segregation: Divided cities in the light of the 2015 "Οχι" referendum in Greece. *City, Culture and Society,* 7(3), pp. 139–148.

Russell, B., 2019. Beyond the local trap: New municipalism and the rise of the fearless cities. *Antipode,* 51(3), pp. 989–1010.

Rutt, R.L. and Gulsrud, N.M., 2016. Green justice in the city: A new agenda for urban green space research in Europe. *Urban Forestry & Urban Greening,* 19, pp. 123–127.

Scanlon, K., Whitehead, C.M.E. and Arrigoitia, M.F., 2014. *Social housing in Europe.* Chichester, West Sussex: Wiley Blackwell.

Taylor, M., 2007 Community participation in the real world: Opportunities and pitfalls in new governance spaces. *Urban Studies,* 44(2), pp. 297–317.

Tsenkova, S. and Polanska, D.V., 2014. Between state and market: Housing policy and housing transformation in post-socialist cities. *GeoJournal,* 79(4), pp. 401–405.

van Holm, E.J., 2019. Unequal cities, unequal participation: The effect of income inequality on civic engagement. *The American Review of Public Administration,* 49(2), pp. 135–144.

Verwiebe, R., Raimund, H., Dorner. J., et al., 2020. *Lebensqualität in einer wachsenden Stadt: Endbericht an die Stadt Wien.* Vienna: University of Vienna.

Wolff, M. and Wiechmann, T., 2018. Urban growth and decline: Europe's shrinking cities in a comparative perspective 1990–2010. *European Urban and Regional Studies,* 25(2), pp. 122–139.

Index

Note: **Bold** page numbers refer to tables; *italic* page numbers refer to figures and page numbers followed by "n" denote endnotes.

accessibility 54, 76, 118, 125, 127
active citizenship 42–46
active labour market policies (ALMPs) 10, 86–90, 92, 93, 111, 152
affordable housing 8–10, 53–66, 68, 69, 71, 73, 75–80, 139, 152; policies 9
Arbeitsmarktservice (AMS) 88, 91, 94–96
austerity 104, 154; policies 2
Austrian People's Party (ÖVP) 21–22, 24, 27, 30, 32, 38, 40

citizen participation 35–37, 39, 42–47, 148
citizenship 6, 63, 64, *64,* 66, 107, 155
city council 19, 22, 24, 38, 118, 121, 123, 124; elections 24, 26
city planning 9, 154
climate change 69, 124, 131, 146, 149, 151, 153, 154
collaborative housing 70, 76–78
COVID-19 pandemic 96, 146, 154

decentralisation 9, 11, 38–39, 41, 46, 74, 86–88, 90, 135, 148, 152
democracy 9, 35, 38, 69, 75, 78, 80, 151, 152, 155
dualisation 4, 54, 55, 59–63, 65, 66, 147, 153, 154

economic competitiveness 1, 8, 39, 110, 146, 151
economic crises 2, 3, 102, 111
education 20, 25, 102–104, 110, 134
elections 19, 20–27, 30–32, 136, 148
employment 86–89, 91, 94–96, 100–106
environmental justice (EJ) 8, 10–12, 117–118, 132–134, 143, 150, 151
environmental policy 134–137
environmental quality 11, 26, 27, 131–143
European cities 1–6, 8, 41, 53, 100–102, 117, 146, 148, 155; justice and 3–6; model 1, 2, 146
European Social Fund 42, 94, 95

financial crisis 1, 2, 76
Flexicurity Law Package 97n4
Fordism 4, 146
Freedom Party of Austria (FPÖ) 20, 21, 24, 27, 28, 32, 39, 44, 58, 59, 148

gentrification 143, 151
global cities 4, 5
global competitiveness 4
global interconnectedness 6
globalisation 32, 100, 148
Greens 4, 21–22, 24–25, 27, 30–32, 124, 148
green spaces 22, 119–122, 124, 126, 127, 131–143; availability 125–127; equity 124, 125, 127

160 *Index*

housing 2, 8; access 9–10, 54–58, 60, 63–66; conditions 54, 58, 59, 61, 63, 65, 66, 68, 70, 74, 79; costs 54, 55, 58, 62–63, 65; markets 9, 63, 65, 142, 143; model 148, 153; policy 10, 37, 53–59, 72; security 54, 56, 59, 61, 63–66, 149; subsidies 55–58, 66, 70, 73, 74; systems 54, 55, 59, 66, 149

immigration 65, 99, 100, 102, 107, 110, 139, 143
income inequality 31, 53, 63, 64
innovation 9–10, 68–69, 74, 75, 80, 147, 152
institutional arrangements 85–97
institutional change 86–87
institutional pathways *40*
institutional responses 6–8

just city 6, 54, 69, 80, 112, 153–155

labour: new divisions of 99–112; transformations 149
labour markets 2, 8, 10, 12, 25, 99, 101, 102, 104, 111, 112, 142, 150; employment and unemployment 102–106; position 134, 138, 139, 142; urban 4
limited-profit housing associations (LPHAs) 55–57, 60, 69–72, 74, 77, 79
Local Agenda 21 Alsergrund 41
low-income groups 63, 64, 66, 149

marginal employment 112n2
migration 30, 53, 63
multi-level governance 2, 3, 11, 20, 21, 25, 31, 85–89, 93, 149, 154–155
municipal housing 56–57, 62, 64, 65, 70–72, 149

Neos 27, 30–32, 148
non-institutional actors 9, 37, 38, 41–43, 46

occupational class composition 106–110
occupational policies 10; restructuring 10

Parity Commission 85, 97n1
participatory urban governance 39
part-time employment 104, 110
planning process 37, 38, 40–42, 45–47, 78, 121
polarisation 4, 99–112, 152; asymmetrical 111, 150; tendencies 106
political participation 4, 7–9, 26, 147–148, 151, 152, 154
population growth 2, 25, 53, 70, 76, 102, 118, 123, 126, 137, 150, 154
professionalisation 99–112, 150, 152
public actors, UGS planning 118–127

quality of life 1, 20, 32, 122, 123, 128, 132, 134, 136

recognition 1, 3, 8–10, 12, 19, 36, 41, 42, 54, 55, 57, 59, 65, 80, 85, 118, 127, 132, 136, 143, 151
red island 19–33
redistribution 1, 8–10, 12, 19, 20, 31, 64–66; redistributive capacities 55, 58, 59, 65, 66, 149, 151, 153, 154; redistributive policies 3, 5, 31, 32, 90
Red Vienna 2, 31, 35, 53–66, 76, 120
rental housing 53, 56, 58, 60, 61, 63; private 58–59, 62, 65; segment 53, 58, 59, 65, 66, 149
rent control 53–56, 58, 59, 63, 65, 66
representation 1, 2, 8, 36, 42, 47, 126, 151, 152
resilience 2, 3, 104, 146–155; approach 5–6; and change 147–151; urban 10

Second World War 1, 7, 55, 70, 96, 120
self-employment 87, 104
self-organisation 43, 44, 46, 78
SMART Housing Program 57, 58, 77, 80
smart city 131, 142; strategy 132, 136–137, 153

social cohesion 1, 77, 80, 110, 146, 151
Social Democratic Party of Austria (SPÖ) 9, 19–22, 24–27, 31–32, 38, 40, 148
social-democratic regime 19, 20; political strength of 20, 25–31
social equity 133, 134, 136
social housing 53, 54, 56–58, 60–64, 66, 68, 69, 73, 75, 77, 79, 80, 149; approaches 68, 78, 80; innovation 68–80; provision 70, 72; subsidised 69–74, 78, 149, 152
social inclusion 2, 3, 53, 96, 99, 131, 152
social inequalities 95, 99, 100, 105, 131–143, 153
socio-economic transformations 7
spatial patterns 20, 26, 27, 31, 117, 123
structural changes 6–8
structural neo-Marxist approach 3–4
sustainability 10–11, 127, 131, 151; social 75, 76

tenants 10, 37, 57, 61, 63, 65, 66, 68, 76, 78, 149, 156; profiles *64*
tenure: restructuring 59–61; security 55, 59–61, 63, 65

Territorial Employment Pacts 89
territorial jurisdictions 8, 147
tertiarisation 100
transitions, challenges 1–12

unemployment 7, 10, 90, 94, 101–106, 112, 150; insurance *91*
urban development 35–47, 39, 41, 43, 44, 118, 119, 121, 122, 123
urban greening 117–128, 143, 150
urban justice 1, 3, 5–9, 11, 36, 53, 54, 69, 75, 77, 78, 80, 146–155
urban transformations 3, 63

Vienna Model 2, 36, 37, 39, 46, 56
votes 20, 24–27, 30–32, 155
vulnerabilities 151–153; social risks 1, 2

welfare: corporatist model 85; federal retrenchment 90–95; Keynesian strategy 58; state recalibration 3; system 4, 20, 31, 85, 87, 93–96, 150, 152
women 76, 89, 104, 106, 110, 111, 121, 139

Taylor & Francis eBooks

www.taylorfrancis.com

A single destination for eBooks from Taylor & Francis with increased functionality and an improved user experience to meet the needs of our customers.

90,000+ eBooks of award-winning academic content in Humanities, Social Science, Science, Technology, Engineering, and Medical written by a global network of editors and authors.

TAYLOR & FRANCIS EBOOKS OFFERS:

A streamlined experience for our library customers

A single point of discovery for all of our eBook content

Improved search and discovery of content at both book and chapter level

REQUEST A FREE TRIAL
support@taylorfrancis.com

For Product Safety Concerns and Information please contact our EU representative GPSR@taylorandfrancis.com
Taylor & Francis Verlag GmbH, Kaufingerstraße 24, 80331 München, Germany

www.ingramcontent.com/pod-product-compliance
Lightning Source LLC
Chambersburg PA
CBHW051746230426
43670CB00012B/2183